THE SECRET OF VICTORIOUS

BLACK

Sergio Junior

By the same author of

Traumas of faith - 12 hours in paradise

I was at your funeral (Before the procession left)

Memories of the Black Lioness

Act and Power - A man against a system

Saved by art

The soul walking in Zigzag - Poems

Firestone - She decided to continue

A mother in despair

THE SECRET OF VICTORIOUS

BLACK

In favor of the promotion of social education and the enhancement of the human figure.

The author would like to thank the association IEME for his financial and cultural support for the production of this work.

This is a work of nonfiction. Names, characters, organizations, places, and situations are not figments of this author's imagination or used as fiction.

"Let us emancipate ourselves from mental slavery, for while others can liberate the body, no one but ourselves can liberate the spirit. The spirit is our only ruler, sovereign."

Marcus Garvey, 1937.

Introduction

The challenges are monumental for those who, in the peak of self-awareness, strive to overcome an external adversary. Yet, the energy required becomes even more substantial, bordering on exhausting, when the objective is to conquer one's own hindrances.

Indeed, every living being, whether in the process of formation, irrespective of skin color or future destiny, is inherently triumphant. This is because the magnificence of life resides within itself, not merely in the vessel it inhabits.

"Dedicate yourself to the good life and consider that each day represents, in essence, a lifetime." - Seneca

Without this intrinsic triumph, there would be neither philosophical nor practical beauty in the existence of gardens, flowers, bees, and butterflies, as all are composed of fleeting brevity.

It is incumbent upon us to scrutinize this system of mirrors and discern who has deprived us of the privilege, even in eras much grander than ours, of perceiving the beauty inherent in our own existence.

Sergio Junior

Preface

Modern life is characterized by a plethora of tasks and constraints that often overwhelm us, leading to the inadvertent neglect of diverse human needs. My friend Sergio Junior's work, "The Secret of the Victorious Blacks," starkly illuminates this oversight.

Consequently, we navigate our existence, steeped in certainties yet burdened by frustrations, wounds, and shortcomings, aligning with the profound wisdom articulated by Carl Gustave Jung: "Until you become conscious, the unconscious will dictate your life, and you will call it destiny."

In this context, it becomes imperative for contemporary authors to raise the alarm about our degradation in terms of genuine humanity. Sergio distinguishes himself as a creative author, facilitating an inner dialogue through texts that are both incisive and gentle.

While there are numerous reasons for me to commend this talented writer, I opt to let you discover the pleasure I experienced in exploring the depths of his work.

Mehdi, Marrakech, Morocco.

THE SECRET OF VICTORIOUS

BLACK

SELF-CONFIDENCE

Men are inherently free, masters of their destiny, transcending attributes like skin color, religion, sexuality, political opinions, or social status. While this should be the prevailing truth, dictatorial rule in certain countries and cultural/historical barriers impose limitations on this assertion. Exploring the annals of ancient and recent civilizations reveals a common thread: the uphill battle for societal establishment and equilibrium. In these collective struggles, individuals, whether through intelligence, strength, or courage, stood out, leaving an indelible mark on their people's history.

History operates actively or passively in all times—past, present, and future—simultaneously.

Embracing this perspective means recognizing the potential to play a role in shaping the ongoing narrative, contributing either as a protagonist or a supporting actor, leaving a lasting legacy like those before us.

Cazuza, the Brazilian singer, encapsulates this temporal continuity in his lyrics: "Time doesn't stop."

The song's essence aligns with the idea that the future often mirrors the past, forming a cyclical pattern.

The philosopher Heraclitus emphasizes the constant flux of everything, akin to a river that is never the same when revisited.

The ever-spinning dice and perpetual motion of time underscore the dynamic nature of existence.

Change, however, comes with sacrifice, and inertia is a precursor to failure. Fragile pretexts and perceptions of difficulty reveal much about an individual's self-evaluation, shaped by their environment, education, and societal systems.

Two pivotal battles emerge in personal, social, educational, and professional development. The internal struggle involves self-perception, influenced by unconscious factors, parental guidance, education, and societal references. A melancholic temperament and aversion to combat intensify this battle, posing challenges to those aspiring to break limiting molds.

The external battle, occurring in the external realm, necessitates persistence, even for those with high self-perception and stable personalities. Defying imposed structures is crucial, as no one else should dictate an individual's place in the world. It's a call to reject puppetry and assert one's desires, avoiding futile struggles against impassable structures that drain energy and compromise independence.

Emphasizing mental health, the message is to free oneself from toxic bonds and social connections that hinder progress. In the face of limiting beliefs, calmly and confidently express dissent, acknowledging one's worth and the pursuit of greater goals.

"Calm is a creative element. It purifies, collects, puts in order the internal forces, compensating for what the disordered movement has dispersed." —Stéphane Zweig.

Leaving voluntarily from situations that don't deserve one's presence, with a clear opinion and a confident smile, signifies liberation and an opportunity to embrace a destiny aligned with one's potential. It's a proclamation that one is born for greater things, deserving respect and a place in the narrative of their choosing.

REFERENCES

In any journey or pursuit, there is a need for both a starting point and a destination. This requirement reflects an understanding of the purpose and objective behind one's actions—whether it be a physical location, a narrative, or an individual who serves as inspiration and motivation for the journey.

The tendency among individuals with dark skin is often to seek references within their own ethnic identity, driven by a profound sense of belonging. While acknowledging and somewhat following this trend as a black person, I am of the opinion that such references should not be confined to parameters like melanin levels, hair types, or eye colors. Categorizing based on these criteria, if taken too literally, perpetuates the division of peoples, introducing a form of segregation that hinders social cohesion instead of fostering unity. It creates divisions when our focus should be on inclusivity.

Despite these considerations, I hold certain beliefs that I do not disavow. In my perception, black skin is among the most beautiful, an opinion that may spark controversy, but it is genuinely what I believe. This perspective is rooted in my upbringing in Salvador-Bahia-Brazil, a predominantly black-brown environment.

While I recognize this as a privilege, I'm aware that not all black individuals share the same experience worldwide.

Many face challenging situations, endure racism, and lack an environment that nurtures high self-esteem.

In response to these challenges, a detached reflection becomes necessary—a perspective untethered from preconceived notions, where truth is considered absolute, and justice universally applied. In this context, the family plays a fundamental role, emphasizing the importance of adequately "preparing the arrow" before launching it into the world.

Children should not be taught to remain silent, lower their heads, and return home emotionally fragile with diminished self-esteem. They require tacit support, motivation, guidance, and encouragement.

My cousin, "Nidinho," becomes a notable figure in this narrative. Josenildo, a black man raised by my determined and encouraging aunt Elione, stood out for his thoughtful and non-robotic approach to life. Despite his elevated level of understanding, which served as a reference point for my mother's comparisons, the emphasis was not on imitating him but rather on adopting the self-assured posture that distinguished him.

Our methods of combat, though deemed morally inappropriate by some, have played a significant role in our societal survival and the assertion of our character. Credit must be given to my mother, whose demanding nature surpassed the norms of her time.

Her commitment to our education, teaching me to read at the age of three, and her strength in handling confrontations at my school underscore her dedication to our success.

In contemplating the metaphorical arrow, I believe it lacks a predetermined destination when launched, much like the unconscious mind. It gains awareness during its journey, influenced by the strength and direction of the initiator, ultimately deciding whether to persist or change course.

The city of Salvador, Bahia, is often referred to as the "Black Rome and Mecca of Negritude," despite Rio de Janeiro and São Paulo ranking higher in terms of black and brown populations. While this designation implies an advantage, it also carries certain prejudices, leading to the deletion or devaluation of references, sometimes unintentionally due to distorted lenses or, at times, envy.

The issue of the deliberate dilution of cultural and referential heritage, replacing them with ephemeral ideas that lack the solidity required to guide a healthier society in the future, personally concerns me. Moreover, the more significant problem across the entire country is the pervasive notion of weakening black individuals, instilling a sense of powerlessness and perpetuating prejudice.

Rather than boosting self-esteem and fortifying intellectual, educational, and cultural capacities, the prevailing mindset diminishes black individuals, limiting their possibilities for success and fostering a perception of social injustice. While I won't delve deeply into this topic now, it is crucial to explore how references are created and transmitted to address these issues effectively and extinguish the metaphorical fire released at the four corners.

HOW DOES THE WORLD KNOW AFRICA?

Have you ever pondered how Africa, with its vast expanse of 30.2million square kilometers, remains largely misunderstood and misrepresented on the global stage?

It's intriguing that schools often omit the fact that Africa is larger than the United States, China, and Brazil combined, constituting 20.4% of the total land area. While Africa's population surpasses 1 billion, it is astonishingly still seen through a lens of misery and poverty, perpetuated by selective media narratives.

Contrary to this prevailing narrative, Africa boasts significant geopolitical and cultural importance. Due to its unique geomorphological characteristics, Africa played a pivotal role in human evolution, remaining less affected during the detachment of continents from the ancient Pangaea.

Holding 30% of the world's oil, gas, and mineral reserves, the continent is abundant in natural resources, with 80% of the population relying on traditional plant-based remedies.

As the home to the majority of the world's youth, Africa is poised to house two and a half billion young people in the next 28 years, constituting almost half of the global population. The continent boasts the second-largest river, the Nile, and the third-largest desert, the Sahara. Additionally, Africa has produced 25 Nobel Prize laureates, with notable contributions in various fields, challenging the stereotype of Africa as a land plagued by curses and misery.

Furthermore, Africa is linguistically diverse, hosting a third of all languages globally—between 1500 and 3000 languages. It holds 60% of the world's wastelands and is home to a significant intellectual force, with 700,000 software engineers contributing to the global tech landscape. Despite these significant contributions, Africa continues to be wronged, facing exploitation by nations and enduring derogatory global propaganda that perpetuates harmful stereotypes.

It's crucial to shed light on this subject as there exists a pervasive mentality that, despite aiming for solidarity and inclusion, inadvertently reinforces feelings of inferiority, intellectual disability, and predisposition to crime among the African (Black) population.

This unfair narrative, akin to viewing Brazil as a jungle populated by Indians who speak Spanish, brands Africa as the "cursed" land or the "pit of misery," requiring a collective awakening.

Historically, Africa has been the cradle of great civilizations, with the Egyptian African Empire creating grand architectural monuments like the Great Pyramid and the Great Sphinx of Giza. The pyramids of Nubia (Sudan) outnumber those in Egypt, while large cities in Zimbabwe and Mozambique thrived with massive stone complexes and castles by the 12th century.

Contributions from Africa extend to mathematics, with the Lebombo Bone dating back to around 35,000 BC. Ancient Egyptians wrote math textbooks over 5,000 years ago, covering concepts still taught in schools today, such as dividing and multiplying fractions.

Beer, baked bread, sandals, toothbrushes and even a pregnancy test (barley sack and hemmer) originated in Africa. And more than that, many inventors who changed world history are Africans:

Gas mask: Garrett Morgan (1914)

Feu tricolore : Garrett Morgan (1923)

Euphonic guitar: Robert Flemming (1886)

Chemotherapy: Jane Cooke Wright (1949)

3D Glasses: Kenneth J. Dunkley (1989)

Transm. Automatic: Richard Spikes (1932)

Beer Tap : Richard Spikes (1908)

Illusion Transm. (film 3D) : Valerie Thomas (1980)

Tampon : Mary Beatrice Davidson Kenner (1956)

Ironing Board : Sarah Boone (1892)

Moreover, Africa has been the birthplace of numerous inventors who have left an indelible mark on world history, challenging the prevailing narrative of despair and victimization.

In understanding these contributions and challenging misinformation, it becomes evident that certain narratives create a distorted image, fueling hatred, sorrow, and divisive arguments.

The realization that black culture is weakened, self-esteem is reduced, and other disadvantages persist due to internalized beliefs is a call for introspection and collective empowerment within the black community.

TOOLBOX

Authentic information, devoid of indoctrination, possesses the transformative power to liberate individuals, transcending ethnic origins. The historical context, when presented in a narrative free from political manipulation, becomes a tool for understanding, breaking limiting beliefs, and formulating public policies that nurture stable identities.

While acknowledging the importance of political engagement, it's crucial to avoid an approach that fosters confrontation and contention. Rather, the emphasis should be on propositional information that solidifies the concepts of overcoming obstacles, encourages mental liberation through education, and utilizes the past as a motivational tool to propel towards a brighter future.

A concern arises from the religious adherence to past grievances, perpetuating a sense of eternal victimhood. This attachment to historical injustices tends to limit the tool set available to the black community, globally, often tethering it exclusively to political debates aimed at rectifying past inequalities.

This approach, however, may divert energy away from preparing for personal success, creating goals, and launching into the world as the protagonist of one's own life. Undoubtedly, historical realities such as slavery and their enduring impacts cannot be denied. Slavery, dating back to 3500 BC in civilizations like Sumerian Mesopotamia, became a widespread institution, leaving deep scars on societies. Yet, it's essential to recognize that, even today, there are more slaves than in any other period in history, highlighting the persistent challenges.

The key lies in steering away from a narrative solely centered on victimhood and engaging in more constructive dialogues. Social residues resulting from historical injustices, like daily discomfort for Black and Brown individuals, are undeniable. However, the focus should shift towards empowering individuals through education, emphasizing the value of intellect and strategic efforts.

Media portrayals and societal biases often perpetuate negative stereotypes, contributing to an environment that associates inferiority with a specific color. While acknowledging the existence of such sick and infected societal attitudes, the emphasis should be on educating people about the value of education and the efficacy of quiet, strategic work.

Instead of relying solely on grievances, it's essential to structure a more coherent and prepared response to the system. Leveraging the lessons from history, particularly those of black individuals who overcame societal limits with intelligence, art, talent, and preparation, becomes a powerful strategy. In the contemporary era of established freedom, there is an opportunity to reflect on the triumphs of those who thrived in more challenging times.

This journey through history can unveil the stories of righteous scholars, geniuses, artists, and intellectuals who defied societal constraints. By highlighting these examples of black excellence, we have the chance to teach our children the possibility of transcending limits and reaching seemingly impossible horizons. The true heroes of history, often overlooked, become a source of inspiration to propel individuals towards intellectual and personal growth.

BLACK INTELLECTUALS

BLACK INTELLECTUALS

Benjamin Banneker

The inspiring story of Benjamin Banneker, an African-American astronomer, watchmaker, and inventor, serves as a remarkable example of intellectual brilliance. Born in 1731 and living until 1806, Banneker utilized his profound knowledge of astronomy to create almanacs that detailed the movements of the Sun, Moon, and planets. Banneker's journey into astronomy and advanced mathematics began with books borrowed from his neighbor, surveyor George Ellicott. Immersing himself in these texts, he started making intricate calculations to predict solar and lunar eclipses. Notably, his work went beyond mere calculations; he even identified and corrected errors made by specialists of his time. Compiling his findings, Banneker created the Benjamin Banneker Almanac, which included a comprehensive chart showcasing the positions of celestial objects and their appearances in the sky at different times throughout the year.

The almanac further provided tide tables for various points in the Chesapeake Bay region. The significance of Banneker's contributions reached beyond national borders. His work caught the attention of Thomas Jefferson, the Secretary of State, who was so impressed that he sent a copy of Banneker's almanac to the Royal Academy of Sciences in Paris. This act was a testament to Banneker's talents and served to challenge prevailing notions of intellectual inferiority ascribed to black individuals during that era. Indeed, Banneker's genius played a pivotal role in shifting perceptions, helping dispel the long-held belief that blacks were intellectually inferior to whites. His story stands as a testament to the power of knowledge, determination, and the ability to challenge societal prejudices.

George Washington sculptor 1864-1943

Absolutely, the story of George Washington Carver is indeed a testament to resilience, innovation, and the impact of education. Born into slavery, Carver overcame immense obstacles to become a pioneering scientist and inventor, best known for his groundbreaking work with peanuts.

Facing adversity in access to education due to racial segregation, Carver's adoptive mother played a crucial role by teaching him to read and write. This early exposure ignited a lifelong passion for learning. Carver, being self-taught, conducted his own biological experiments, showcasing his innate brilliance.

Carver's academic journey led him to earn a master's degree from the botany program at Iowa State Agricultural College. His significant contributions, however, extended far beyond the academic realm. At the Tuskegee Normal and Industrial Institute for Negroes, Carver revolutionized southern agriculture by developing innovative crop rotation methods.

His approach educated farmers on the importance of alternating soil-depleting cotton crops with enriching crops like peanuts, peas, soybeans, sweet potatoes, and walnuts. Carver's practical inventions, totaling over 100 ways to monetize various crops, made farming more profitable and less reliant on cotton.

Carver's influence reached the highest echelons of power. He became an advisor on agricultural matters to President Theodore Roosevelt, and was recognized internationally as a member of the British Royal Society of Arts in 1916.

Remarkably, Carver chose not to patent or profit from his numerous creations. Instead, he freely shared his discoveries with humanity, emphasizing the altruistic nature of his work.

George Washington Carver's legacy endures as that of a great soul who, through his intellect, compassion, and contributions, left an indelible mark on science and society.

Marie Jackson 1921-2005

Mary Jackson's story is an incredible testament to determination, resilience, and breaking barriers. Born in Hampton, Virginia, in 1921, Mary Jackson faced the challenges of racial and gender discrimination during her pursuit of a career in engineering. After earning a double degree in mathematics and physical sciences in 1942, Jackson began her career as a teacher. In 1951, she joined the National Advisory Committee for Aeronautics (NACA), which later became NASA, as a "human computer" working under Dorothy Vaughan. This position involved complex calculations done by hand before the advent of electronic computers.

Despite her remarkable skills and contributions, Jackson faced institutional barriers to career advancement. In 1953, she moved to work on the Supersonic Pressure Tunnel project with engineer Kazimierz Czarnecki. The movie "Hidden Figures" captures a poignant moment in Jackson's life when she addresses the issue of racial and genders discrimination in her pursuit of becoming an engineer.

Facing the requirement for a graduate degree for promotion, Jackson confronted the fact that the University of Virginia, the only school offering graduate engineering courses, did not admit black students at the time. Through her determination, she took legal action, ultimately winning the right to attend the segregated school and earning her graduate degree. In 1958, Mary Jackson became NASA's first black female engineer, breaking through racial and gender barriers in the aerospace industry. Recognizing the challenges faced by the younger generation, she later transitioned to become the federal director of the women's program at Langley. In this role, she worked to create more opportunities for women at NASA.

Mary Jackson retired in 1985, leaving behind a legacy of courage, intelligence, and dedication. Her contributions to the advancement of women and minorities in science and engineering have had a lasting impact, and she continues to inspire future generations.

Annie Easley 1933-2011

Absolutely, let's continue celebrating the remarkable contributions of women in the field of science and technology. Another inspiring figure is Annie Easley, whose achievements in mathematics, programming, and space engineering have left an indelible mark. Annie Easley was a mathematician, computer scientist, and aerospace engineer who worked at NASA. Born on April 23, 1933, in Birmingham, Alabama, Easley faced the challenges of racial and gender discrimination during her time. Raised by a single mother, she pursued her education against the odds and became a trailblazer in the STEM (science, technology, engineering, and mathematics) fields.

Easley began her career at NASA's Lewis Research Center (now Glenn Research Center) in 1955 as a human computer. This role involved performing complex calculations to support various research projects. Over the years, she transitioned into programming and contributed significantly to the development of software for Centaur, the upper-stage rocket used in various space programs.

Her work extended beyond rocketry, and Easley conducted important research in the field of alternative energy sources. Her dedication and expertise were crucial to the success of numerous programs at NASA. Throughout her 34-year career, Easley faced challenges as one of the few African-American employees in her division but remained focused on her job and her passion for science and technology.

Annie Easley's legacy goes beyond her technical contributions. She became an advocate for diversity and inclusion, breaking down barriers for women and people of color in STEM fields. After her retirement in 1989, Easley remained active in promoting STEM education through outreach programs. She continued to inspire and encourage the next generation of scientists and engineers.

Her story emphasizes the importance of perseverance, passion, and a commitment to making a positive impact, regardless of the obstacles faced. Annie Easley's contributions have left an enduring legacy, and her journey serves as an inspiration for aspiring scientists and engineers around the world.

Mae Jemison 1956-

Mae Carol Jemison was born during a time when NASA restricted women from becoming astronauts, particularly impacting the aspirations of Black women. However, Jemison, armed with degrees in chemical engineering from Stanford University and medicine from Cornell University, defied these limitations. In June 1987, she achieved a remarkable feat by being selected for NASA's astronaut program. Just five years later, her dream materialized as she became a crew member aboard the space shuttle Endeavor for the STS-47 Space lab-J mission. This U.S.-Japan cooperative endeavor encompassed 44 experiments in life sciences and materials processing. Jemison, serving as a bone cell experiment researcher at Space lab, contributed significantly to the mission. By the mission's conclusion, Jemison had logged an impressive 190 hours, 30 minutes, and 23 seconds spent in space.

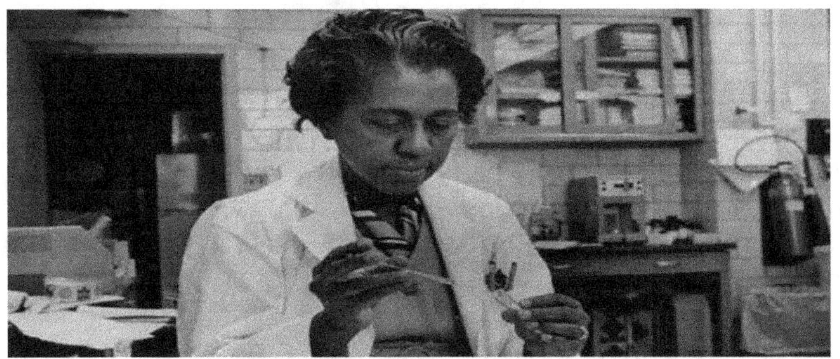

Marie Maynard Daly 1921-2003

Marie Maynard Daly stands as a powerful figure in the galaxies of scientific achievement. As the first Black woman to earn a doctorate in chemistry in the United States, she pioneered groundbreaking research on the effects of cholesterol and sugar on the heart. Born at a time when minority women faced educational and employment restrictions, Daly defied these limitations. In 1942, she graduated with honors in chemistry from Queens College in New York, followed by earning a master's degree in chemistry just a year later. During her tenure as a physician at Columbia University, Daly made a significant discovery related to internally produced compounds aiding digestion. Throughout her teaching career, she dedicated extensive research to cell nuclei, unraveling crucial insights. Daly's contributions extended to her discovery of the link between high cholesterol and clogged arteries, significantly advancing studies on heart disease. In addition, she delved into the effects of sugar on arteries and explored the impact of smoking on lung tissue.

BIG ONES
PERSONALITIES
BLACK

BLACK PERSONALITIES

Frederick Douglass

Born into slavery in 1818, this young man seized a clandestine opportunity to learn how to read, igniting his social and political awareness in the fight against his oppressive condition.

By the age of 20, he successfully escaped enslavement and joined the abolitionist movement. Renowned for his eloquence, he captivated audiences with his oratory skills during meetings and through three autobiographical stories published between 1845 and 1892) that became bestsellers. At every stage of his life, he dedicated himself to introducing fellow oppressed black individuals to the power of reading, education, and emancipatory ideas.

From teaching fellow slaves to read to sharing his own experiences through writing and publishing an abolitionist journal, his influence extended to delivering impactful conferences in Europe. In 1863, following the abolition of slavery in the United States by President Abraham Lincoln, he assumed significant political roles. He fervently campaigned for the adoption of the 13th, 14th, and 15th amendments to the Constitution—ensuring the abolition of slavery, defining citizenship, and prohibiting the denial of voting rights based on race and color.

Today, he stands as a pioneer of black activism and a key architect of the abolition of slavery. We owe to him the establishment of "Black History Month," a period inviting everyone to honor the "often neglected accomplishments of Black Americans," as proclaimed by President Gerald Ford in 1976. It's also noteworthy that Frederick Douglass shares the same birth month with Abraham Lincoln, the Republican president who left an indelible mark on history.

CARL BRASHEAR, 1931–2006

Carl Maxie Brashear, born on January 19, 1931, in Thionville, Kentucky, achieved historic milestones as the first African-American Master Diver in the United States Navy in 1970. His remarkable life story was portrayed in the 2000 film "Men of Honor," featuring Cuba Gooding, Jr.

Despite being born into poverty on a small farm, Brashear harbored ambitions of becoming a Navy sailor. He attended Sonora Grade School from 1937 to 1946. Brashear enlisted in the U.S. Navy on February 25, 1948, and graduated from the U.S. Navy Diving and Salvage School in 1954, officially becoming a Navy diver. Notably, he was the first African

American to graduate from this school and the first black diver officer in the Navy. Brashear faced a significant challenge during the Palomares Incident in January 1966 when he was tasked with helping recover a lost nuclear bomb off the coast of Palomares, Spain. During the recovery, a towing line broke, leading to severe damage to Brashear's leg, resulting in its amputation below the knee. Despite facing persistent infections and necrosis, Brashear, in 1968, became the first amputee reinstated as a diver.

In 1970, he achieved the historic feat of becoming the first African-American Master Diver in the U.S. Navy and continued to serve for over a decade, ultimately reaching the rank of Master Diver. Brashear retired on April 1, 1979, as Commander-in-Chief, later working as a civilian government employee at Naval Station Norfolk until his retirement in 1993. Cuba Gooding Jr. portrayed Brashear in the film "Men of Honor," which depicted his inspiring life story.

Carl Brashear passed away on July 25, 2006, at the age of 75, due to respiratory arrest and heart failure at Portsmouth Naval Medical Center, Portsmouth, Virginia. He was laid to rest at Woodlawn Memorial Gardens, Norfolk, Virginia. Following his death, his sons established the Carl Brashear Foundation in his honor. Brashear received the Secretary of Defense Medal for Outstanding Public Service in October 2000, recognizing his 42 years of military and federal civilian service. Additionally, on October 24, 2007, the Newport News Fire Department dedicated a 35-foot high-speed boat named after Carl Brashear for use by marine incident response team divers.

Malcolm X

Malcolm, violent rights of the black community. He refused assimilation and said:

"I don't see the American dream, only the American nightmare."

It must be remembered that his father was lynched by the Ku Klux Klan when he was five years old, that he was separated from his mother and that he turned to delinquency before coming to this cause of liberation of the black man. Malcolm

Their goal was to protect blacks against police abuses by forming militias. Angela Davis will be part of it, but she did not agree with everything, including the idea of creating an African-American nation separate from the United States.

Rosa Parks

Rosa Louise Parks, born in 1913, is revered as one of the key figures in the civil rights movement in the United States. Descended from slaves, Parks faced the daily deprivations imposed on black people during her childhood, notably having to relinquish her seat on the bus to white passengers, as dictated by segregation laws. However, her refusal to yield her seat to a white man on December 1, 1955, led to her arrest, trial, and charges of public disorder and violation of local laws. Parks' courageous stand triggered a nationwide wave of protests, culminating in significant changes to the country's segregation laws. Born in 1913, she attended various schools until she entered Alabama State Teachers College High School, affiliated with Alabama State University.

Her educational journey faced interruptions as she took on responsibilities caring for her grandmother and ailing mother, delaying her high school diploma until 1934. During the 1930s, Parks emerged as an activist for the NAACP (National Association for the Advancement of Colored People). Serving as a secretary and youth leader for the association, she was in the midst of organizing an NAACP youth conference at the time of her arrest.

In response to her arrest, Montgomery's black population initiated a boycott of the city's buses that lasted over a year, marking one of the early instances of direct action in the civil rights movement.

Despite not receiving a formal degree during her lifetime, Rosa Parks earned forty-three honorary doctorates in recognition of her activism. Numerous universities, including Florida State University and Soka University in Japan, conferred these honorary titles. Troy State University – Montgomery presently houses the Rosa Parks Library in her memory. Rosa Parks passed away in October 2005 at the age of 92.

Martin Luther King Jr. 1929–1968.

Certainly, Martin Luther King Jr. is an iconic figure in American history, renowned for his pivotal role as a leader in the civil rights movement. An American Baptist minister and political activist, he spearheaded nonviolent and civil disobedience actions to advocate for political rights and combat racial segregation and discrimination.

King's influence was instrumental in pivotal events such as the Montgomery bus boycott in 1955, which he led, and his presidency of the Southern Christian Leadership Conference (SCLC). His efforts extended to organizing nonviolent protests in Birmingham in 1963 and the historic March on Washington, where he delivered the famous **"I Have a Dream"** speech.

In recognition of his commitment to combating racism through nonviolent means, King was awarded the Nobel Peace Prize in 1964. His activism evolved to address broader issues, including poverty and opposition to the Vietnam War. However, his endeavors drew the attention of the FBI, led by J. Edgar Hoover, who considered King a radical and subjected him to the counterintelligence program.

Tragically, King was assassinated on April 4, 1968, in Memphis, just as he was planning the Poor People's Campaign, an occupation of Washington, D.C. His death triggered widespread demonstrations, and allegations of involvement by government agents persisted for years.

In his honor, Martin Luther King Day was established as a public holiday in the United States, starting in 1971, and federally recognized by President Ronald Reagan in 1986. King's legacy lives on through numerous roads and a county named in his honor.

The journey of these remarkable individuals, including Rosa Parks, Frederick Douglass, Benjamin Banneker, Carver, and many others, indeed reflects stories of resilience, courage, and determination against challenging circumstances. Their enduring legacy continues to inspire generations to come. So, take a moment, have a coffee, and let's continue this journey.

ENEDINA ALVES MARQUES

Enedina Alves Marques (1913-1981) stands as a pioneering figure in Brazilian history, breaking barriers and challenging societal norms to become the first woman to graduate in engineering in the state of Paraná and the first black woman engineer in Brazil.

Born into a black family that had migrated from rural areas after the abolition of slavery, Enedina's pursuit of education began at a young age when she worked for a military intellectual and republican, Domingos Nascimento, in exchange for a school education. Despite facing numerous challenges, including financial constraints and societal expectations, she became literate at the age of 12 and enrolled in the Paraná Education Institute in 1926. Enedina's tenacity led her to work as a servant and nanny for Curitiba's elite to fund her studies. She obtained her teaching diploma in 1932 and taught in various public schools in Paraná between 1932 and 1935. However, her dream was to become a civil engineer.

Returning to Curitiba, Enedina overcame significant obstacles to earn her degree in civil engineering from the University of Paraná (now the Federal University of Paraná) in 1945, making her the first woman with higher education in the state and the first female engineer in Brazil.

As the sole woman in her class, Enedina navigated a post-abolitionist society that lacked public policies and opportunities for upward mobility for the black population. She faced both gender and racial prejudice in a predominantly white region. Undeterred, she became an assistant engineer at the Paraná State Secretariat for Transportation and Public Works in 1946 and later transferred to the Department of Water and Power.

Enedina contributed to significant projects in the state, including the Capivari-Cachoeira Power Plant and the construction of the Paraná State College. Known for her energetic and rigorous work style, she gained respect in a male-dominated field, often wearing overalls and carrying a pistol at her waist for self-protection.

In the 1950s and 1960s, Enedina expanded her horizons by traveling the world. She became one of the beneficiaries of Major Domingos Nascimento's will in 1958. Immortalized as the "pioneer of engineering," her legacy is honored in the Mulher Memorial in Curitiba. Enedina Alves Marques passed away in 1981 at the age of 68, leaving an enduring impact on Brazil's engineering landscape. In her honor, the Instituto de

Mulheres Negras Enedina Alves Marques was established to combat racial invisibility in various sectors, advocating for black men and women's rights in education, the labor market, and other social spheres. Despite her passing, Enedina continues to be remembered through tributes, with streets and institutions named after her, acknowledging her remarkable contributions to Brazilian engineering and society.

Luís Gonzaga Pinto da Gama, 1830 – 1882

Luís Gama's life is indeed a remarkable and inspiring story of resilience, intellect, and dedication to the abolitionist cause in 19th-century Brazil. Born to a free black mother and a white father, Gama faced the harsh reality of being sold into slavery at the age of 10 due to his father's debts.

Gama's journey from slavery to becoming a renowned lawyer and abolitionist is a testament to his determination and intelligence.

Despite being illiterate until the age of 17, he won his freedom through the courts and went on to educate himself. His commitment to the abolitionist cause led him to work as a lawyer on behalf of captives, and by the age of 29, he had already established himself as a prominent author and abolitionist.

The historical erasure you mention, where Gama's name is not mentioned in some works, underscores the challenges faced by black intellectuals in having their contributions recognized and acknowledged. This erasure has been a longstanding issue, and it's crucial to shed light on individuals like Luís Gama, who played a significant role in the fight against slavery.

Despite his pivotal role in advocating for abolition and the end of the monarchy in Brazil, Gama passed away six years before these causes were realized. His posthumous recognition in the Steel Book of National Heroes in 2018 reflects the acknowledgment of his contributions to Brazilian history.

The mid-19th century context of São Paulo, where Gama spent much of his life, adds depth to understanding the challenges and dynamics of the time. The city's transition from a provincial capital to a hub for coffee production influenced the economic landscape and the value of urban property, including slaves.

Gama's early life, his mother's participation in the Sabinada Revolt, and his sale into slavery due to his father's debts are heartbreaking episodes that highlight the harsh realities faced by many during that period.

The stigma associated with captives from Bahia, as a result of the Malês Revolt, further emphasizes the racial biases and prejudices prevalent at the time.

The ambiguity surrounding Gama's birth details, including the absence of his father's name in his account, raises questions about identity and the challenges faced by individuals in asserting their freedom. His journey from being a domestic slave to a literate and self-educated man, enlisting in the army and working towards his freedom, showcases his resourcefulness and determination.

Luís Gama's story is an essential part of Brazil's history, highlighting the struggles and triumphs of black intellectuals in the fight against slavery and injustice. His legacy continues to inspire those advocating for social justice and the recognition of marginalized voices in historical narratives. Luís Gama's life continues to unfold as a remarkable tale of activism, literary achievement, and legal prowess. His efforts in the abolitionist cause are particularly striking, and his multifaceted contributions to Brazilian society are truly inspiring.

Gama's time in the municipal guard, his imprisonment for insubordination, and his marriage to Claudine Fortunata Sampaio, reveal a complex and dynamic life. Despite facing adversity, his skills in reading and writing set him apart from many other slaves, enabling him to secure positions such as a copyist for official authorities and a clerk in the São Paulo Police Department. His decision to pursue a legal education, even facing opposition from college students, showcases his determination. Gama's method of studying alone and attending classes as a listener, eventually earning the title of "déliré," reflects his commitment to gaining legal knowledge independently.

The challenges and opposition he faced during his time as a legal practitioner, especially in slave cases, ultimately led to his dismissal from the police department in 1868. Gama's resignation, described as for the "good of public service," underscores his commitment to the abolitionist cause and his refusal to compromise his principles.

His literary work, "Primeiras Trovas Burlescas," highlights Gama's intellectual and creative abilities. This collection of poems, dedicated to Salvador Furtado de Mendonça, also includes works by his friend José Bonifácio, o Moço. Despite facing obstacles, Gama's literary contributions secured him a place in Brazil's literary pantheon.

The estimate that Gama had already freed more than 500 slaves and his involvement in the "Questão Netto" case, where he secured the freedom of 217 slaves, underscore his significant impact on the abolitionist movement. The famous phrase attributed to him during a jury trial, defending the idea that a slave who kills his master does so in self-defense, adds to the mystique surrounding Gama's legacy. While there is debate about the origin of this particular quote, its powerful message resonates with the broader themes of Gama's advocacy for freedom and justice.

Gama's ability to articulate profound concepts is evident in his defense of four slaves labeled as "four Spartacus" who had murdered the son of their master. The idea that the slave who kills the master is fulfilling an inevitable prescription of natural law is a powerful assertion that challenges prevailing notions of justice and morality.

The controversies surrounding specific quotes attributed to Gama do not diminish the overall impact of his work and advocacy. His legacy endures as a symbol of resilience, intellectual prowess, and unwavering commitment to the fight against slavery and injustice in 19th-century Brazil.

Luís Gama's legacy continued to reverberate even after his death, with his funeral becoming a significant and emotionally charged event in the history of São Paulo. The details surrounding his passing and the subsequent funeral shed light on the profound impact he had on the community and the admiration he garnered. Gama's battle against slavery and his relentless pursuit of justice had earned him the title of a great abolitionist and slave liberator. His death on August 24, 1882, marked the end of an era, but the funeral procession that followed turned into a monumental event, reflecting the deep respect and appreciation for his contributions. Raul Pompeia, a contemporary abolitionist, noted Gama's declining health before his death. Gama had been suffering from diabetes, and in the morning of August 24, 1882, he lost the ability to speak. Despite the intervention of over 20 doctors, Gama succumbed to his illness that afternoon.

The funeral procession became a symbolic and emotional tribute to Gama's life and work. The streets were filled with mourners, both men and women, expressing their grief. His body, placed on a stretcher in the front room, had its face cast in plaster by a sculptor, preserving his visage for posterity.

The original plan to transport Gama's body to the cemetery in a funeral carriage was thwarted by the overwhelming crowds. Gama, known as "the friend of all," was to be carried by the people themselves. The business closed its doors, and flowers were thrown at the coffin as a mark of respect.

The funeral procession, led by friends and supporters of the deceased, made its way through the city. The crowd that followed the bier was immense, with people vying for the honor of carrying the coffin. The hearse, among a plethora of cars, remained empty in a poignant symbol of the profound loss. The procession encountered a fanfare in Brás and received the support of the Irmandade de Nossa Senhora dos Remédios on Ladeira do Carmo.

As it passed through the town, shops closed their doors, flags were hoisted at half-mast, and the people, both mourning and watching, crowded the streets. Families gathered at windows to pay their respects. The funeral became a spectacle, and speeches interrupted the procession, emphasizing the widespread impact of Luís Gama's life and the depth of admiration he commanded.

The funeral was a significant event in the history of São Paulo, marked by an outpouring of emotion and respect for a man whose legacy continued to inspire generations. In the words of various observers across different periods, Luís Gama's funeral was an unprecedented spectacle, the largest known at the time, and a profoundly moving event in the history of the city of São Paulo.

Luís Gama's impact and legacy extended far beyond his lifetime, leaving an indelible mark on Brazilian history and the ongoing struggle for freedom and equality. The details of the events and tributes following his death highlight the enduring significance of his contributions. The account of Gama's funeral procession reflects the unity of people from all social classes, with both a slave owner and a "poor black man in tatters and bare feet" carrying the beer, symbolizing a moment of shared respect for the abolitionist leader.

The speech at Gama's grave, led by individuals like Doctor Clímaco Barbosa or Antônio Bento, emphasized the importance of preserving the ideas for which Gama fought. The crowd, in a powerful moment, took an oath together, promising not to let the ideals die. This marked the transition from a legalistic phase of the abolitionist movement to more direct actions against slave owners, as seen in the invasion of Chácara Pari and the sheltering of runaway slaves.

Gama's grave, purchased on the same day as the burial, became a symbol of his lasting impact. The commitment made at his gravesite marked the beginning of a new phase in the abolitionist movement, characterized by effective actions against slavery.

Posthumous tributes and recognitions continued to honor Gama's memory. The founding of the Luís Gama Lodge by the São Paulo Freemasons, the appearance of the newspaper Getulino in Campinas paying homage to Gama, and the erection of a bust in his memory in Largo do Arouche highlighted the ongoing influence of his ideas.

In modern times, Gama's story has been explored in various forms of media, from literature like Ana Maria Gonçalves's "Um Defeito de Cor" to plays like "Luís Gama - A Voice for Freedom," and the film "Doctor Gama" released in 2021. The University of São Paulo posthumously awarded him the title of doctor honoris causa in 2021, recognizing his significant contributions.

The Brazilian Bar, São Paulo section, also granted him the title of lawyer 133 years after his death, acknowledging his role as a legal figure in the abolitionist movement. The unprecedented tribute ceremony, titled "Luiz Gama: Ideas and Legacy of the Abolitionist Leader," showcased the enduring importance of Gama's fight for freedom, equality, and respect.

These tributes and recognitions across different forms of media and institutions underscore the lasting impact of Luís Gama's life and ideas on the ongoing struggle for justice and equality in Brazil.

BLACK ARTISTS

BLACK MUSICIANS AND ARTISTS

Ray Charles Robinson, Albany, 1930 – 2004

Ray Charles, born Ray Charles Robinson, was indeed a legendary figure in American music, known for his exceptional talent and innovation in soul, blues, and jazz. His impact on the music industry is profound, and he is celebrated as one of the greatest singers and musical artists of all time.

Ray Charles's decision to shorten his name when entering the entertainment industry, avoiding confusion with the famous boxer Sugar Ray Robinson, marked the beginning of a career that would redefine the landscape of American music. He played a crucial role in introducing the gospel rhythm to R&B music, leaving an indelible mark on the evolving sounds of the late 1950s. Voted by Rolling Stone as the 2nd greatest singer of all time and the 10th greatest musical artist of all time, Ray Charles's contributions spanned various genres, making him a versatile and influential figure. His ability to blend elements of R&B, gospel, and jazz in songs like "I Got a Woman," "What I'd Say," and "Hit the Road Jack" paved the way for the soul music of the 1960s.

Ray Charles's early life, marked by blindness at the age of seven, did not hinder his musical journey. He attended the St. Augustine School for the Blind and Deaf, where he honed his skills in music, particularly excelling at the piano. Despite facing personal tragedies, including the loss of his mother and father during his teenage years, he continued to pursue his passion for music.

Throughout his career, Ray Charles demonstrated versatility, coexisting with various musical genres such as jazz and country. Hits like "Unchain My Heart," "Georgia On My Mind," and "I Can't Stop Loving You" showcase his ability to convey emotion and connect with audiences on a deep level.

Despite challenges, including struggles with drug problems, Ray Charles's live performances continued to captivate audiences. His unique talent and recognized genius were evident in every song he sang, making him a revered star in American pop music.

Ray Charles's legacy endures through his timeless music, and his influence on subsequent generations of musicians remains palpable. The acknowledgment of his genius and the celebration of his contributions to music attest to the lasting impact of this iconic artist.

Stevie Wonder, 13 May 1950

Stevie Wonder, born Stevland Hardaway Morris, is an iconic American singer, songwriter, and activist known for his exceptional contributions to soul, blues, and jazz music. Renowned as one of the greatest contemporary musicians, Wonder has left an indelible mark on the music industry.

Stevie Wonder's journey in music began at a very young age when he was signed to Tamla Records, a Motown Records label, at the age of eleven. Over the years, he has recorded over thirty top ten hits and has won an impressive twenty-five Grammy Awards, making him the male artist with the most Grammy wins in history. Born as Stevland Hardaway Judkins, Wonder faced challenges in his early life, including blindness caused by retinopathy of prematurity. Raised by his mother, Lula Mae Hardaway, in Detroit, Wonder showed a remarkable talent for playing various instruments, including piano, harmonica, drums, and bass, during his childhood. His involvement in a church choir reflected his early connection to music.

At the age of 18, Stevie Wonder moved to Los Angeles, where he collaborated with producers like Quincy Jones. His breakthrough came at the age of 13 with the hit "Fingertips (Pt. 2)," showcasing his vocal and instrumental prowess. Eventually, he gained creative control and rights to his own songs when negotiating with Motown, marking a significant turning point in his career. The 1970s marked Stevie Wonder's classic period, and albums like "Music of My Mind" and "Talking Book" showcased his thematic and musically explorative approach. Superstition and You Are the Sunshine of My Life from "Talking Book" were massive hits, earning three Grammy Awards each.

In 1973, Stevie Wonder experienced a serious car accident, resulting in a coma for four days. Despite partial loss of smell and temporary loss of taste, he returned to the stage, demonstrating resilience and determination in his musical journey. Throughout the 1980s, Wonder continued to create timeless music, and the album "Stevie Wonder's Original Musiquarium" in 1982 included new classics like "Do I Do" and "Ribbon in the Sky." His collaboration with Paul McCartney on "Ebony and Ivory" and participation in Michael Jackson's "Bad" album showcased his enduring influence. Stevie Wonder's impact on music extends beyond his artistic achievements. His activism for humanitarian and social causes has solidified his status as a cultural and social icon. With a career spanning decades, Stevie Wonder remains a beloved and influential figure in the world of music.

Louis Daniel Armstrong, New Orleans, 1901–1971

Nicknamed "Satchmo", "Satch" and "Pops", he was an American musician and singer. He is considered one of the most influential and important figures in jazz, with a long career spanning five decades, being renowned for his talents as a trumpeter, cornetist and saxophonist.

Armstrong was born into a very poor family. He spent his youth in poverty in a section of New Orleans known as "the back of town." His father, William Armstrong, left the family when Louis was still a child and married another woman. His mother, Mary Albert Armstrong, left Louis with his aunt, uncle and grandmother. At the age of five, he returned to live with his mother and rarely saw his father.

He was at the Fisk School for Boys where he first came into contact with music. He brought some money home as a paperboy and traveling shoemaker. However, this was not enough to keep her mother away from prostitution. He began sneaking into music bars near his home to hear and see the singers.

He experienced very difficult days, and he considered his youth as the worst time of his life and, sometimes, he even drew inspiration from them: "Every time I close my eyes while blowing my trumpet, I look straight in the heart of good old New Orleans... It gave me a reason to live."

"Every time I close my eyes while playing my trumpet, I look straight into the heart of good old New Orleans... It gave me a reason to live."

He managed to buy a trumpet, with money borrowed from a Russian Jewish immigrant family, the Karnofskys, whom he considered until the end of his life as members of his family since they took care of him several days and nights, while his mother worked. For this reason, Louis wore a Star of David for the rest of his life.

After dropping out of Fisk School at age 11, Armstrong formed a quartet that played on the streets to earn money, and by this time he was also starting to get into trouble.

Cornet player Bunk Johnson taught him to play by ear at "Dago Tony's Town" in New Orleans, although Louis credited a musician named Oliver in later years. Armstrong strongly developed his trumpet playing in the band of the institution

"New Orleans Home for Colored Waifs", where he was sentenced to 11 years for shooting a pistol in the street during a New Year's celebration, after having been sentenced to 18 months in prison. Professor Peter Davis established discipline and provided the boy with a musical education. Eventually, Davis made Armstrong the band's leader.

"Home" played throughout New Orleans and the 13-year-old began to gain attention for his trumpet playing, beginning a new musical career. At 14, he left the group and lived with his father and his new stepmother, then with his mother on the street. Armstrong got his first night job at Henry Ponce's, where Black Benny became his protector and guardian. He burned coal in the factory during the day and played the trumpet at night.

He frequently played in Brass Band Parades and listened to the older players whenever he could, learning from Bunk Johnson, Buddy Petit, Kid Ory and, especially, Joe "King" Oliver, who acted as a mentor and father figure For the young. Musician man. He later played on the riverboats of New Orleans, working with Fate Marable on the Mississippi. He described his time with Marable as "going to college", which provided him with a unique experience.

On March 19, 1918, Satchmo (Armstrong's nickname) married Daisy Parker of Gretna, Louisiana. They adopted a three-year-old child, Clarence Armstrong, whose mother, Louis' cousin Flora, died in childbirth. Clarence Armstrong was mentally ill (the result of a stroke at an early age) and

Louis would spend the rest of his life caring for her. Louis divorced Daisy and soon after she died.

During his riverboat experiences, Armstrong's music began to mature. By the age of twenty, he already knew how to read sheet music and began playing large, extended trumpet solos, being one of the first jazz players to do so and introducing his personality and style into his solo turns. He had just learned to create a unique sound and began singing in his performances. In 1922, Armstrong traveled to Chicago at the invitation of Joe "King" Oliver to join his "Creole Jazz Band" where he earned enough without having to perform in the old nightclubs. Chicago, the Windy City, was populated by many blacks who, after working in factories, had money to spend on going to bars.

Armstrong lived in Chicago in his own apartment, which had a bathroom (the first in his life). Excited to find himself in this city, he began writing nostalgic letters to his friends in New Orleans. As Armstrong's career grew, he was challenged to participate in "cutting contests" (competitions in which one musician tries to steal another's work by playing better than him) by men who were trying to put an end to the new phenomenon. However, they all failed. Armstrong made his first recordings on the Gennett and Okeh labels (jazz records began to explode across the country), including a few solos and breaks, while he was second trumpet in Oliver's band in 1923. Around this time he met Hoagy Carmichael (with whom he later collaborated) who was introduced by Bix Beiderbecke, his friend, who now owned his Chicago Band.

His second wife, pianist Lil Hardin Armstrong, helped Armstrong develop his new style away from Oliver. She convinced her husband to play classical music in churches to perfect his style, and to try performing without an orchestra and in a church choir. Lil's influence ultimately determined the relationship between Armstrong and his mentor, particularly when it came to salary and bonuses that Oliver hid from him and the other band members. The group broke up in 1924 and Armstrong was invited to New York to play with the Fletcher Henderson Orchestra, the most successful African-American group of the era. Louis learned to play in an orchestra for the first time.

Armstrong quickly adapted to Henderson's more controlled style, and other musicians quickly adopted Armstrong as an emotional and natural player. During this time Armstrong made several recordings, arranged by his old friend from New Orleans, pianist Clarence Williams, these included concerts of the Williams Blue Five (in which Armstrong joined), solos of jazz and a series of accompaniments with blues players. Artists such as Bessie Smith, Ma Rainey and Alberta Hunter. Armstrong returned to Chicago in 1925 because of his wife, who wanted to encourage him to pursue his career. He really liked New York and admitted that the Henderson Orchestra was quite limited. He began recording under his own name with the famous Hot Five and Hot Seven, producing big hits like Potato Head Blues, Muggles (a reference to marijuana) and West End Blues.

The band included Kid Ory (trombone), Johnny Dodds (clarinet), Johnny St. Cyr (banjo), Armstrong's wife, and generally no drummer. Of Armstrong, St. Cyr said, "We felt so relaxed working with him...he always did his best to present each individual." His recordings with pianist Earl Fatha Hines and Armstrong's introduction to West End Blues remain the most famous influences in jazz history. Armstrong was now free to develop his personal style as he saw fit.

Armstrong also performed with Erskine Tate's Little Symphony, at the Théâtre Vendôme. They provided music for silent films and live performances, including versions of classical "jazz" music including Madame Butterfly, which gave Armstrong experience of new types of music and performing in front of a large audience. They became the most famous jazz group in the United States. After splitting from Lil, Armstrong began performing at the Sunset café for Joe Glaser, an associate of Al Capone. In the Carroll Dickerson Orchestra, with Earl Hines on piano, which quickly morphed into Louis Armstrong's Stompers, Armstrong formed a lifelong friendship with Hines and led, for the first time, a musical group.

Armstrong returned to New York in 1929, where he played in the orchestra of the musical Hot Chocolate and made an appearance in Charles John's band Dégonia. He began working at Connie's Inn in Harlem, the second most famous nightclub in the Big Apple. Armstrong also had considerable success with vocal recordings, including versions of famous songs composed by his old friend Hoagy Carmichael. His 1930 recordings took full advantage of the "ribbon microphone" (chest microphone) over all other band recordings of the era, albeit at lower quality. The most famous was Stardust, which remains one of Armstrong's most profitable recordings to this day. The Great Depression of the 1930s hit jazz hard. Bix Beiderbecke died and Fletcher Henderson's band disbanded.

Many musicians stopped playing nightclubs, and some stopped being musicians. King Oliver made a few recordings, but they were not successful. Sidney Bechet became a tailor, and Kid Ory returned to New Orleans to raise chickens. Armstrong moved to Los Angeles in 1930 in search of new opportunities. He played at the New Cotton Club in L.A. with Lionel Hampton on drums. In 1931, Armstrong appeared in his first film: Ex-Flame. He returned to Chicago in December 1931 and played in the groups of Guy Lombardo and Raphaël Minsby where he was remembered by the public.

He traveled to almost every state, and in March 1934 he returned to New Orleans, where he received a hero's welcome. Furthermore, he sponsored a local basketball team, Armstrong's Secret Nine, and named a type of cigarette after him. But soon after, he hit the road again and was forgotten again, prompting him to flee to Europe. In 1967, he recorded What a Wonderful World, perhaps the song most associated with Armstrong.

At the time, he was criticized by black American activists for not being more actively militant in the civil rights movement. However, it must be remembered that at this time, Louis was already approaching 60 years old and belonged to a different generation than that which was at the forefront of protests and activism at the end of the 1950s and throughout the 1960s. In recent years, Armstrong became an artist who fought for civil rights, although he used his art as a means to do so.

Robert Nesta Marley, Bob Marley Nine Mile, 1945-1981

He was a Jamaican singer and songwriter, the most famous reggae musician of all time, famous for popularizing the genre internationally. Marley sold more than 75 million records, and in 1978, three years before his death, he received the Third World Peace Medal from the United Nations. His work mainly focused on political, social and spiritual themes. Dedicated to protesting social injustice, Bob Marley is celebrated around the world as the voice of the poor and oppressed, and is considered a symbol of black resistance, spirituality and the fight for social justice.

His songs denounce racism, social inequalities, colonialism and war. A follower of the Rastafarian religious movement,

Bob Marley's life and work were deeply influenced by his faith. His music has served as a spokesperson for the beliefs and themes of the Rastafarian faith, such as Afrocentric interpretations of the Bible and Pan-Africanism. Africa and its problems, such as poverty and European colonization, were also widely discussed topics in their songs.

The Legend compilation, released three years after his death, which brings together some of the artist's least militant songs, is the best-selling reggae album in history. Bob was married to Rita Marley (from 1966 until his death), one of the I Threes, a trio of backing vocalists who continued to sing with The Wailers, Marley's band, after the group achieved international success. She was the mother of four of her twelve children (two of whom were adopted), such as the famous Ziggy Marley and Stephen Marley.

Other of his children have also pursued musical careers, such as Ky-Mani Marley, Julian Marley and Damian Marley. Bob Marley was named the 11th greatest musical artist of all time by Rolling Stone Magazine.

Bob Marley was born on February 6, 1945, in Nine Mile, a village located in the Jamaican parish of St. Ann, in the interior of the country. The artist was the son of Norval Sinclair Marley, a captain in the English, Jamaican and White armies, aged 50, born at May Pen, Clarendon, of English descent from Sussex County, and of Cedella Booker, a young woman of eighteen years old. , poor and black, also born in Nine Mile.

Cedella and Norval were due to marry on July 9, 1944, however, Norval did not marry and left her pregnant, having returned to England. He did not know his famous son Bob Marley, who after becoming an adult, discovered he had a paternal half-sister, Constance Marley, whom his father had when he returned to England and married. The singer's father died of a heart attack in 1955.

That same year, his mother married Toddy Livingstone, a black Jamaican, also from Nine Mile. In search of a better life, Bob Marley moved with his mother and stepfather to the country's capital, Kingston, going to live in Trench town, Jamaica's largest and most miserable slum, where Bob Marley suffered bullying, shunned **by local blacks for being black, light-skinned and** have a small size.

 In 1964, Bob Marley's maternal half-sister, Claudette Pearl Livingstone, was born. Bob was raised with Bunny Wailer, born April 10, 1947, his stepfather's son, who became his best friend and considered him a brother.

When he moved to Trench town, Bob was still young and already had a strong connection to music. He and his best friend Bunny, his father-in-law's son, improvise tin guitars and play hits from America, particularly New Orleans, connected to a mini transistor. They captured Ray Charles, Fats Domino, Brook Benton (one of Marley's favorites) and bands like the Drifters, who were very popular in Jamaica.

By the early 1960s, the R&B movement began to decline in the United States, and it was becoming difficult to acquire records to satisfy the insatiable diet of releases that the

Jamaican people demanded. The owners of Sound Systems were then forced to invest in the talent of local musicians. Around this time, music was beginning to develop on the island that incorporated Jamaican musical traditions with R&B and big band influences, resulting in the vibrant and eventful sound of ska. Jamaica's independence in 1962, ceasing to be a British colony, helped create the moment for the creation of an original Jamaican music.

The owners of Sound Systems then became producers. They rented a two-story studio, found a young man with a talent for singing about his emotions, lived in the ghettos of Kingston, and recorded ska records.

When Bob Marley left school at 14, he seemed to have only one ambition: music. But, to please his mother, who feared he would become a rude boy (as juvenile delinquents are called in Jamaica), he got a job as a welder.

He spent his free time with Bunny, honing his vocal skills. They were aided by one of Trench town's most famous residents at the time, singer Joe Higgs, who gave informal singing lessons to aspiring artists who wanted to hone their skills. It was at one of these sessions that Bob and Bunny Wailer met Peter Tosh, another young man with great musical ambition.

In 1962, Bob auditioned for producer Leslie Kong, who released his first recordings. "Judge Not, composed by Marley himself, was the first. Although the songs recorded were not played on the radio and attracted little public attention, they confirmed Marley's ambition to become a singer.

The following year, he decided the way forward was to start a band. He joined with his friends Bunny Wailer and Peter Tosh to form the Wailing Wailers. They chose that name for the group because they said that when you're born in the ghetto, you're born to moan, and "moan" means "to moan." The new group had a mentor: a Rasta percussionist named Alvin Patterson, who introduced the boys to producer Coxsone Dodd. In the summer of 1963, Coxsone heard the Wailing Wailers and, satisfied with the group's sound, decided to record them.

The Wailing Wailers completed their first single, Simmer Down on Coxsone's label, in the final weeks of 1963. By January of the following year, it was number one on the Jamaican charts, and it held that position for two following months.

The group, Bob, Bunny and Peter, with another singer, Junior Braithwaite and two backing vocalists, Beverly Kelso and Cherry Smith, headlined the Jamaican scene. "Simmer Down" became a sensation on the island, and the Wailing Wailers began recording regularly for Coxsone Dodd's legendary Studio One. The group now created themes identifying with the Rude Boys of the streets of Kingston. Jamaican music had finally an identity and someone who spoke the purest language of the ghetto.

In the following years, Marley's group recorded a few additional hits in the island's charts, which established the group's popularity, but, despite this, the economic difficulties they were going through meant that Junior Braithwaite, Beverly Kelso and Cherry Smith left the group. .

In 1965, Bob's mother separated from Toddy Livingstone and in 1966 she married Edward Booker, a white American military civilian. Both moved to Delaware, with Pear Livingstone, Cedella Booker's then two-year-old daughter. Bob Marley continued to live in Kingston, Jamaica, and did not want to move with his mother, half-sister, and new stepfather.

Cedella insisted that he move in with them and save money to send young Marley, then 21, a plane ticket. Bob's mother's intention was for him to start a new life there, where he would have more opportunities. Before agreeing to move to the United States, Bob met a young woman named Rita Anderson, and on February 10, 1966, they were married.

Marley's stay in the United States with his wife was short-lived. They lived in Bob's father-in-law's house, and the artist worked in the countryside as a waiter to finance his true professional ambition: to be a musician. In October 1966, Bob Marley, after eight months in Delaware, returned to Jamaica with his wife.

This was a decisive period in its formation, as the Emperor of Ethiopia, Haile Selassie, had made a state visit to Jamaica in April of that year, and during the period Bob was away the Rastafarian movement took on a new life in the streets. From Kingston. Marley began to delve deeper and deeper into the Rastafarian spirit and culture.

By 1967, Bob's music already reflected his new conviction. Rather than singing anthems for the Rudes Boys, Marley began composing social and spiritual themes, which became his trademark and greatest legacy. He teamed up again with Peter Tosh and Bunny Wailer to reorganize the group. They simplified the original name "Wailing Wailers" to "The Wailers". Rita had started her career as a singer and had achieved great success with the song Pied Piper, a cover of an English pop song. Jamaican music, as far as she was concerned, was changing: the upbeat ska had been replaced by a slower, more sensual rhythm called steady rock.

In the late 1960s and early 1970s, the Wailers also teamed up with studio wizard Lee Perry, who transformed the technical possibilities of recording into an exquisite art form. The Wailers' union with Lee Perry resulted in some of the group's finest productions. Tracks like Soul Rebel, Duppy Conqueror, 400 Years and Small Ax were not only classics, but set the direction of reggae. Despite local acclaim, the group remained obscure internationally.

In the summer of 1971, however, Bob accepted an invitation from Johnny Nash to accompany him to Sweden, where the American singer was commissioned to produce the soundtrack for a Swedish film. While in Europe, Marley signed a deal with CBS, which of course was also Nash's label. In the summer of 1972, all the Wailers were in London, ostensibly promoting a single for CBS: Reggae on Broadway. But like Nash's film, the project failed and the Wailers found themselves in hot water in a faraway land. On his final

European move that year, Marley visited the Island Records studios in London and asked if he could see founder Chris Blackwell.

Chris Blackwell, a white Jamaican, of English descent, from a wealthy and traditional island family, had founded Island Records in Jamaica in the late 1950s and was already involved in Jamaican musical culture, even before the days of Ska . The company was one of the pioneers in the export of Jamaican music to the world and in the 1960s became primarily responsible for the distribution and promotion of the island's music in the United Kingdom, from ska to rocksteady to reggae. So when Marley made his first move to the island in 1971, he connected with the hottest independent label of the time.

Blackwell knew of Marley's reputation on the Caribbean island. Both from the side in which they were known as a gang of Rude Boys, and that they were of unparalleled quality and fiber and that, above all, they were very popular and respected both in Jamaica and, already at the time, throughout the Caribbean. The group was offered a trust offer where Chris Blackwell, the contractor, gave an advance of £4,000 (approximately US$8,000), and carte blanche for them to travel to Jamaica and produce material for the Wailers' debut album on Island Records.

For the first time, a reggae band had this kind of treatment, comparable to their rock 'n roll contemporaries, with access to the highest level of recording. Before that, reggae was considered to only sell low-cost singles and compilations.

Blackwell was warned by several people not to trust the boys so much, and that perhaps registered with the money without seeing the result of any registration. After a few months, the Wailers were back in London with material they had recorded at Island Studios in Kingston.

To make the material more pleasing to the ears of international audiences, guitar solos and keyboard lines performed by English musicians were added to the original recordings. Blackwell's strategy was to launch the Wailers as a new rock band, made up of black Jamaicans. The result was the album Catch a Fire, with suggestive packaging in the shape of a lighter, from which the vinyl is removed by opening the cover.

The record was heavily promoted, leading to the rise of Bob Marley's international success and recognition. Marley's cadence, combined with his lyrics of peace, protest and social commitment, was a complete contrast to what was happening in the rock scene at the time. The label decided that the Wailers should tour the UK and US, again a complete novelty for a reggae band. They embarked on a tour of Europe, which solidified their live appearances. Bob Marley returned to Jamaica in 1978. The musician decided to give a free concert in Kingston to celebrate his return. On April 22, 1978, Bob Marley & The Wailers performed at the National Stadium in Kingston in the famous One Love Peace Concert. In this broadcast, Marley called on then Jamaican Prime Minister Michael Manley, leader of the PNP party, and Edward Seaga, leader of the opposition party, to join hands and swear an oath of peace. The crowd attending the concert went wild. Bob Marley and the band left for the United States, where they played two concerts at Madison Square Garden. During the second presentation, he became ill on stage and began to investigate what was happening with the reggae idol. Although having health problems, he even played one more concert in Pittsburgh, on September 23, 1980 (Bob Marley's last concert), but soon the world learned the sad news that the reggae star was suffering from a type of skin cancer called acral lentiginous melanoma, one of several types of melanoma, that has developed on the nail of the big toe. Doctors advised him to amputate the finger, but Marley refused to do so because of his Rastafarian philosophy, which holds that the body is a temple that no one can change (which is why Rastas grow beards and dreadlocks). He was also concerned about the impact of the operation on his dancing; the amputation would profoundly affect his career when he was at its peak.

The cancer has spread to his brain, lungs and stomach. He battled the illness for eight months, seeking treatment from Dr. Joseph Issels in Germany in late 1980 and early 1981. For a time, Marley's condition seemed to have stabilized thanks to the German doctor's naturalistic treatment. In May 1981, when Dr. Joseph Issels announced that there was nothing more to be done, Bob Marley, already overcome by illness, decided to return home to Jamaica to spend his last days with his family and friends. He was unable to complete the trip, having to be admitted to a Miami hospital. He died just before noon on May 11, 1981, less than 40 hours after leaving Germany.

BLACK ATHLETES

BLACK ATHLETES

FRANCIS NGANNOU

Ngannou was born in the small town of Batié, Cameroon. At the age of six, he saw his parents separate and moved in with relatives with his mother, three brothers and sister. His father abandoned the family, leaving a tarnished reputation that affected the children. ***" He had a bad reputation. People saw me and said I would be like him. I hated it, I felt a lot of shame"***, says Ngannou, noting that his father was a street fighter who often had problems with the police. Francis always had a desire to fight, inspired by his idol Mike Tyson. However, his circumstances did not yet allow him to dream. At the age of 12, Ngannou began working in a sand mine. Batié didn't have a gym for him to train in, so at age 22 he began pursuing his dream by moving to Douala, where he also practiced boxing while working in a clothing factory . It wasn't enough. He realized that staying there wouldn't get him anywhere, so he decided to try his luck in Europe.

"My journey began with a trip from Cameroon to Morocco, which lasted almost a year. It was a year of living illegally, crossing borders, living in the bush, eating garbage. A terrible life," said he told Bleacher Report. From Morocco, he tried to enter Spain, but was immediately arrested and spent two months in prison.

"It was more stressful than scary. When we arrived in Spain, we were pretty relaxed, even in prison. We knew we were going to be arrested, but then we would be released," he says. Once released, he went to France. Without money, he moved to Paris at age 26 and became homeless.

"Compared to what I experienced until I arrived in Morocco, sleeping in a parking lot was like being in a five-star hotel," he recalls. Ngannou immediately did three things: figure out where to find food, find a place to sleep, and find a boxing gym. The Cameroonian asked strangers for information, found a promising gym and spoke to the coach, asking to train.

"I just moved. I have nowhere to live, and I have no money, but I'm not here to ask for favors. I just need a place to train because I'm going to be world champion," he said. With a height of 1.93 meters, he was impressed, he won 50 euros to buy clothes and a backpack. Oddly enough, just when his boxing dream seemed closer, the situation completely changed.

The coach and teammates began to suggest that he should try his hand at mixed martial arts (MMA) – "but what is MMA?", Ngannou asked. He learned and heard about another place: the Lopez MMA Factory. The owner, Fernand Lopez, was also from Cameroon, and the connection was immediate. He offered new equipment and a roof over his head. Ngannou started living in the gym. Francis always insisted on training in boxing until his first MMA fights, and he enjoyed it. Ngannou started with five wins and one loss.

He liked it and earned enough money to get his own place. Ngannou became so good that it was difficult to find opponents for him. First in France, then throughout Europe, no one wanted to face someone of his size and strength. In 2015, he got the biggest opportunity of his life; a contract with the UFC. His first fight was against Luis Henrique KLB. A knockout. He had 10 wins in the UFC, nine by knockout and one by submission, and two losses, until the second chance at the championship – the first ended in a disappointing loss to Stipe Miocic in 2018.

However, this weekend, the story was completely different and turned into a real fairy tale. With a brutal knockout, Francis Ngannou became the UFC heavyweight champion. After eating garbage and living on the streets, Ngannou is now on top of the world. And few will have the audacity to want to dethrone him from there!

Jesse Owens, 1913 – 1980

The American sprinter was the first athlete in history to win four gold medals at the same Olympic Games.

Owens won the 100 and 200 meters, the long jump and the 4 × 100 relay. But this did not happen in any edition of the Olympic Games, but at the 1936 Games, in Berlin, within Nazi Germany, in front of Adolf Hitler.

The athlete shocked not only the Germans, but also the Americans, who at that time lived under strong segregationist laws. His story became a film, called "Race."

Aïda dos Santos

In the photo, Aïda carries the Olympic torch at the 2016 Brazilian Olympic Games. Aída dos Santos Menezes (Rio de Janeiro, March 1, 1937) is a former Brazilian athlete, specialist in high jump.

She was born prematurely, the youngest of six siblings, the daughter of an alcoholic bricklayer and a washerwoman. He lived with his family in Morro do Arroz, a slum in Niterói. Discovered by Fluminense, in the first competition she won, she was beaten by her father, who said that a medal does not fill the stomach. When I was at Vasco, I didn't go to training because I used the ticket money to buy food. To go to college, I went to class in the morning, worked in the afternoon, and worked out in the evening. He has a degree in geography, physical education and pedagogy. From 1975 to 1987 she was a professor of physical education at the Federal University of Fluminense (UFF).

Participation in two editions of the Olympic Games. In Tokyo in 1964, he finished fourth in the high jump, reaching the mark of 1.74 m. During this edition of the Games, Aída was the only woman in the Brazilian delegation. No structure was provided to her: she traveled without a technician and without equipment to compete. He didn't even have clothes for the opening ceremony: he wore a uniform adapted from another competition. Still, she became the first woman in Brazil to compete in an Olympic final. Four years later, at the Mexico Games, he placed twentieth in the pentathlon.

She is the mother of volleyball player Valeska Menezes, with an institute to promote social inclusion through athletics and volleyball. In 2006, Aída dos Santos received the Adhemar Ferreira da Silva Trophy from the Brazilian Olympic Prize and in 2009 she received the World Diploma for Women and Sport, a special award from the International Olympic Committee.

Mohamed Ali 1942-2016

Considered by many to be the greatest boxer of all time. Ali was world champion in the heavyweight category, Olympic champion in the light heavyweight category and, in professional boxing, he had a total of 61 fights with 56 victories and only five defeats.

Born Cassius Clay, the athlete became Muhammad Ali when he converted to Islam. The boxer joined the organization known as the Black Islamist, which fought for the rights of black Americans. In 1967, Muhammad Ali refused to fight in the Vietnam War, was banned from competing in boxing for three years and had his heavyweight belt stripped.

MIKE TYSON

Mike Tyson, whose full name is Michael Gerard Tyson, known as Iron Mike, (former American Boxer born June 30, 1966, in Brooklyn, New York, United States), became the youngest heavyweight champion in history at the age of 20 years.

He was a member of various street gangs from a young age, he was sent to a reformatory in upstate New York in 1978. In this reformatory, the social worker and boxing enthusiast Bobby Stewart recognized his potential for boxing and referred him to renowned trainer Cus D'Amato, who became his legal guardian. Tyson became a professional boxer in 1985. D'Amato taught Tyson a "peek-a-boo" style of boxing, with boxing gloves held close to the cheeks, tightly clenched fists and a continuous swinging motion in the boxing ring that made his defense almost impenetrable. At 1.78 m tall and weighing around 100 kg, Tyson was short and stocky and did not have the appearance of a classic heavyweight boxer, but his speed in his sequence and his surprising aggression in the ring surpassed most of his opponents. On March 6, 1985, Mike Tyson made his very first fight against Hector Mercedes, which he won in the first round after one minute and 47 seconds of combat. Only one just over a year later, on November 22, 1986, he became the youngest heavyweight champion in professional boxing history, with a second-round knockout over Trevor Berbick, to win the World Boxing Council (WBC) belt.). On March 7, 1987, he acquired the World Boxing Association (WBA) belt by defeating James Smith. After defeating Tony Tucker on August 1, 1987, Mike Tyson was unanimously recognized as champion by all three organizations (WBC, WBA and the International Boxing Federation [IBF]).

After the deaths of D'Amato and manager Jimmy Jacobs, Mike Tyson signed with controversial promoter Don King. He successfully defended his world heavyweight title ten times, including against former champions Larry Holmes and Michael Spinks. In 1988, Tyson married actress Robin Givens, but the couple divorced in 1989 based on allegations that Mike Tyson physically abused her. A myriad of assault and harassment accusations were subsequently made against Tyson. On February 11, 1990, in one of the greatest upsets in English boxing history, Mike Tyson lost his world title to little-regarded challenger James ("Buster") Douglas, who inflicted a technical knockout in the 10th round (Tyson was undefeated in 37 boxing fights at that time). Tyson bounced back from that loss by winning four straight. In 1991, however, he was accused of raping beauty pageant contestant Desiree Washington and he was convicted of this charge in 1992.

After his release from prison in 1995, boxing champion Mike Tyson returned to boxing and in 1996, at a world championship boxing event, he regained two of his championship belts with easy victories over Frank Bruno and Bruce Seldon.

On November 9, 1996, in a long-awaited fight with two-time heavyweight champion Evander Holyfield, Tyson lost for the second time in his professional career, by a technical knockout in the 11th round. During the rematch against Holyfield on June 28, 1997, he was disqualified after twice biting his opponent's ear and, as a result, lost his boxing license.

"I just want to do what I do best, and that's fight. I love that." -___ Mike Tyson

Tyson was eventually granted a new license, and he returned to the ring on January 16, 1999, when he defeated Franz Botha in the fifth round. On February 6, however, this great champion was sentenced to one year in prison, two years of probation and 200 hours of community service and was fined $2,500 after pleading no contest to the charges according to who assaulted two elderly men following a car accident in 1998. Tyson was released after serving only a few months of the one-year sentence.

Nevertheless, Tyson's self-control problems continued. After the referee broke up a fight in June 2000 with American Lou Savarese, Tyson continued to throw punches and inadvertently injured the referee. In comments made to the press after that fight, Tyson outraged boxing fans with bizarre and vicious remarks about British heavyweight champion Lennox Lewis. In his October 2000 fight with Andrew Golota, Tyson won in the third round, but the fight was later declared "canceled" because Tyson tested positive for marijuana. Tyson only had one other fight between October 2000 and his June 2002 fight with Lewis.

It had been difficult to schedule this fight. The two men were contractually tied to different promoters and cable television companies. Tyson had attacked and bitten Lewis during a press conference, which also had a dampening effect. Tyson's legal troubles resulted in him being denied a boxing license by the United States sanctioning bodies that usually organize major boxing matches (such as Nevada). It had been so long since Tyson had fought a boxer of his caliber that no one knew the level of his skills. The matter was settled when Lewis knocked out Tyson twice during the fight before defeating him for good in the eighth round. "If I retire, it is above all to no longer bring shame to boxing." Tyson scored his last professional victory in 2003, a 49-second first-round knockout.

Later that year, he filed for bankruptcy, reporting he was $34 million in debt after earning a fortune of around $400 million during his career. Tyson lost fights in 2004 and 2005, and he retired following the latter fight. In 2007, he spent 24 hours in jail after pleading guilty to drug possession and driving under the influence, charges that stemmed from a 2006 arrest.

To this day, Mike Tyson remains for all fans of the noble art a reference, a legend and the boxer with the biggest punch in the history of boxing. He is also an inspiration to many professional and amateur boxers. Before becoming professional, Mike Tyson made 54 amateur boxing fights for 48 victories and six defeats. 58 professional fights: 50 victories (44 KO), 6 defeats and 2 fights without decisions

Youngest world heavyweight boxing champion at 20 years, 4 months and 23 days

First boxer to reunify the different world heavyweight belts, 16 world championships contested (12 victories for 4 defeats)

2-time WBC world heavyweight champion

2-time WBA world heavyweight champion

2-time IBF heavyweight world champion

In this video, we have selected for you the 10 most beautiful knockouts of Mike Tyson's career.

He made more money than Michael Jordan. Well, sort of. In 1990, Tyson became the highest paid athlete in the world, including Michael Jordan. He made $28.6 million in 1990. Michael Jordan, on the other hand, made "only" $8.1 million that year. He holds an honorary doctorate. In 1989, Tyson received an honorary doctorate from Central State University. Ironically, Tyson never graduated from high school. According to the-Central State University President Arthur Thomas, "Mike demonstrates that hard work, determination and perseverance can overcome any obstacle."

He has a tattoo of Chairman Mao. While Tyson was in prison, he wished he had been placed in solitary confinement so he could read Mao's communist writings. He respected Mao so much that he got a tattoo of him on his bicep. He converted to Islam in prison. Finally, when Tyson was in prison, he had a lot of time to think. This led him to convert to Islam in prison, and he even changed his name to Malik Abdul Aziz.

He was sober for five years. Tyson believed that having sex before a boxing match would make him weak, so for five years he refused to have sex. This is not a new concept, however; many fighters think the same thing as Iron Mike. He revealed that he was cheating doping controls. Indeed, in 2019, Iron Mike admitted that he used his sons' urine to thwart authorities' anti-doping controls. The personal and professional exploits of former world champion Mike Tyson were chronicled in the documentary Tyson, which premiered at the Cannes Film Festival in 2008, and in a one-man show, Mike Tyson: Undisputed Truth, which he first performed in Las Vegas in 2012. (The show was later staged on Broadway in a production directed by filmmaker Spike Lee). He has also starred in several television shows and films, including the hit comedy The Hangover (2009) and its sequel (2011), as well as the animated television show Mike Tyson Mysteries (2014-), a parody of the different Scooby-Doo cartoon series. His memoirs Undisputed Truth (2013) and Iron Ambition: My Life with Cus D'Amato (2017) were co-written with Larry Sloman. Mike Tyson was inducted into the International Boxing Hall of Fame in 2011. Mike Tyson being a boxing legend, he is now often invited to the media and does not hesitate to give his opinion on new boxers.

Serena Williams

Black Quebeau, dynamic and talented, you have undoubtedly seen him on TV. Serena is, among all active tennis players, the athlete who holds the most Grand Slam tournaments in singles, doubles and mixed doubles. She is also the third tennis player to stay at the top of the world rankings for more weeks.

Additionally, he has won four Olympic gold medals, three in doubles and one in singles. Serena Williams is the highest-paid tennis player in history. She has a career winning rate of 85%, having played in over 1,200 matches.

James Lebron

Currently, it is the leading NBA name. Considered by many to be the successor to Michael Jordan, LeBron has been truly influential in the basketball league since his debut in 2003. The owner of three NBA championship rings and two Olympic gold medals, James collects sure achievements on and in outside the field.

LeBron was the first black man and the third man in history to grace the cover of Vogue magazine. The athlete has a foundation called the LeBron James Family Foundation, which is headquartered in Akron, Cleveland.

In 2015, it entered into a partnership with the University of Akron to provide scholarships to up to 2,300 young people starting in 2021. In 2018, the foundation, with the city of Akron, created the I Promise School, a school that, in addition to teaching, helps fight against school dropouts.

According to Lebron, the creation of the school was the greatest achievement of his life.

The player has previously stated several times that he feels it is necessary to use his status to position himself and draw attention to racial and humanitarian causes. It's about having status, and that takes talent and work.

USAIN STORE

Usain St. Leo Bolt, OJ, OD (Trelawny, 21/08/1986)

BOLT is a former Jamaican sprinter, multiple Olympic and world champion in this modality. After retiring as a sprinter in 2017, he debuted as a football player. He is the only athlete in history to become a three-time champion in two track modalities at the Olympic Games consecutively (100 meters and 200 meters) and also two consecutive champions in the 4 x 100 meters relay modality.

He is the only athlete to have won eight gold medals in sprint events, being a ten-time world champion. Considered the fastest man in the world and his feats in athletics led him to be nicknamed Lightning Bolt by the international press.

Among the many awards he has received, the most impressive are the IAAF Athlete of the Year and the Laureus

World Sport Award for Male Athlete of the Year, which he received four times. Among the honors he has received outside of athletics are the Order of Jamaica (OJ) and the Order of Distinction (OD), awarded by the Jamaican Government. The highest paid athlete in the history of athletics, receiving $20.3 million per year according to Forbes, he is considered by Jacques Rogge, former president of the International Olympic Committee, by experts and by former athletes, as a living legend of the sport. And the greatest sprinter of all time.

Lewis Hamilton

Particularly inclined towards Brazil because of his admiration for Ayrton Senna, which he does not hide from anyone, he is the first and only black driver in Formula 1, and no less than seven times world champion in the category.

Englishman Hamilton is considered by many to be the greatest name in the history of motorsport.

In 2020, he surpassed Michael Schumacher's winning mark, something few believed possible. He is also the second-youngest driver to become world champion in the category.

During the last contract renewal, in 2018, Hamilton became the highest paid driver in Formula 1 history.

Michael Jordan, was a great American basketball player, is a living legend of sport in the world. Jordan brought a spark of genius to professional basketball's greatest league, the NBA, to another level. And he is certainly one of the people responsible for popularizing the sport outside the United States. Influenced children and adults are spread across the most diverse places in the world.

He is the titleholder:

6 times NBA champion;

Five were once named the best players of the season.

6 times the best player in the final; basketball (player who scores the most points) in the championship in ten seasons;

Two time Olympic champion and at the Barcelona Olympics (1992) he was part of the best basketball team in history. Certainly the king of basketball courts. It would be like a basketball kick.

In addition to being an accomplished basketball player, Jordan was also a leader on the court. Being good at what you do and continuing to inspire people around the world is something few people can do with such mastery.

In basketball there is a situation called "Clutch Time", which corresponds to the moment when the clock is close to zero, surely one of the moments of greatest pressure. After all, a basket can bring victory or lead to defeat.

On several occasions, the team trusted Jordan for the last "kick", they knew it was decisive. This is because he was a player with great precision power. To succeed and have the trust of our team, we must always be ready. To be so specific, Jordan relentlessly qualifies this offer. He was the first to arrive and the last to leave. Focus and dedication can maximize the chances of achieving the success you want.

Until he became the greatest basketball player in history, Michael Jordan trained a lot. And after becoming the greatest, he continued to train.

Just because you performed well doesn't mean you already know everything there is to know. There is still much to discover and improve. Remaining in the search for constant qualification is the best strategy to be more competitive. Keep in mind that there is always something you can improve on.

Michael said in a commercial that he missed more than 9,000 shots, lost more than 300 games, and missed 26 times in which his team gave him the "winning kick. But he overcame all those mistakes. And he never gave up, he kept going, training and surpassing himself. What differentiates those who achieve their goals and those who give up is how they react to mistakes. Some become discouraged and give up, others use error to find the right path and achieve victory.

Michael Jordan was the leader of the brilliant Chicago Bulls team, the group that won the NBA trophy six times. The team was known as the "dream team" and although Jordan had a lot of responsibility, he knew how to recognize the importance of the team. As the popular saying goes, one swallow doesn't make a summer. Relying on a good team is essential for any leadership.

The team had excellent players who were committed and aligned to achieve a common goal. In this way, Jordan worked for the team as the link between the group and the dream of being champion. ***I can accept failure. Everyone fails at something. But I can't accept not trying.*** *Michael Jordan*
And we're running out of space to talk about our world-famous athlete, Pelé. It would take another book just to talk about it.

Edson Arantes do Nascimento, Three hearts,**1940-2022**

Better known as Pelé, he was a Brazilian footballer who played as a striker. Described as the "King of Football", he is widely considered the greatest athlete of all time.

In 2000, he was named Player of the Century by the International Federation of Football History and Statistics (IFFHS) and was one of two co-winners of the FIFA World Player of the Year award. That same year, Pelé was elected Athlete of the Century by the International Olympic Committee. According to the IFFHS, he is the second-highest scorer in the history of football in official matches, having scored 765 goals in 812 matches. In total there are 1283 goals in 1363 matches (including unofficial friendlies), a Guinness World Record. During his career, he became the highest paid athlete in the world for a time.

Sadio Mane

Sadio Mané is a Senegalese footballer born on April 10, 1992, in the village of Bambali, near Sédhiou. He plays as a winger and center forward for Bayern Munich.

Born in Bambali, in a rural community in southern Senegal, Sadio Mané quickly became a football fan. He has great admiration for the Brazilian footballer Ronaldinho and the Senegalese international El-Hadji Diouf, whom he considers his role models. To anyone who had the opportunity to see him play, it was clear that this feisty little boy was way above standard. It was clear that he was destined to be a great player in the future. However, this vision was unfortunately not to everyone's taste. Indeed, Sadio's father, who was none other than the village imam, and whose severity was almost proverbial throughout the region, took a very dim view of the fact that his son was more interested in football. than his school learning.

He did not hesitate to reprimand him with a belt to dissuade him from playing. However, the punishments inflicted by his father will not be the most persuasive. Little Sadio will do as he pleases, and will continue to play with his friends in secret. As he reaches adolescence, Sadio will aspire to more independence. He wanted to make his dream of becoming a professional footballer come true at all costs. So, he will run away to try his luck in the Senegalese capital, Dakar.

"I fled the village to go to Dakar, without anyone knowing. And a week later, while they were looking for me everywhere, they knew that I was in the capital and then brought me back to the village."
Seeing that his beloved son was willing to do anything to achieve his goal, including putting himself in danger by traveling alone and without resources, Sadio's father finally

came to accept his passion for football. Mané convinces his people to let him leave the village to meet trainers in town. He goes to Mbour, the largest football city in Senegal, with his precarious equipment (shorts and damaged shoes).

In 2018, Mané made a check worth 234,000 euros available to his native village, to help finance the construction of a high school and offered 300 jerseys from his club (at the time) Liverpool FC to his village. African football has given birth to many legends, and it is clear that the African continent is a veritable cornucopia of young talents. The young Senegalese is considered today as one of the best players of his generation, and his legendary dribbling has helped give him a reputation as a great technician.

ACTORS

Samuel L. Jackson was born on December 21, 1948, in Washington, D.C. His career is marked by an impressive list of successful films, and he has become one of the most recognizable and respected actors in the film industry. Samuel Leroy Jackson grew up in Chattanooga, Tennessee. He was raised by his mother and maternal grandparents, his family being involved in the civil rights movement. He attended historically black institutions, including Morehouse College in Atlanta, Georgia, where he studied zoology. After becoming involved in the civil rights movement in the 1960s, Jackson became aware of his interest in drama. He then began his career in theater and appeared in Broadway productions. His first film appearance took place in the film "Together for Days" in 1972.

In the 1980s, Samuel L. Jackson struggled with drug and alcohol problems, which impacted his career. However, he managed to overcome these difficulties and recover. He resumed his career on stage and obtained roles in notable productions like "Soldier's Play."

Jackson's real breakthrough came in the 1990s. His association with director Spike Lee was particularly fruitful, with memorable roles in films such as "Jungle Fever" (1991) and "Do the Right Thing" (1989). He also played in "Pulp Fiction" (1994) by Quentin Tarantino, which earned him an Oscar nomination.

Since the 1990s, Samuel L. Jackson has appeared in numerous successful films, becoming an iconic figure in the Hollywood film industry. Some of his most memorable roles include Mace Windu in the Star Wars prequel trilogy, Jules Winnfieldin "Pulp Fiction", Nick Fury in the Marvel Cinematic Universe, and many more. In addition to his acting career, Samuel L. Jackson is also a civil rights advocate and has actively participated in social causes. He has supported organizations such as the NAACP Foundation, which fights racial discrimination. Samuel L. Jackson has a reputation as one of the most versatile and talented actors of his generation. His exceptional career, charismatic presence and commitment to social causes make him a respected figure both in the film industry and beyond.

Denzel Washington made a nice speech while speaking to his friend Samuel L. Jackson at the 12th Governors Awards:

"We go back so far, but I'll start with 152 **movie titles**. I have IMDb Pro. (audience laughter) 152 film titles, 27 billion in box office revenue. 27 billion, more than any other actor in history, Samuel L. Jackson. Eleven times, Nick Fury. Once, Django. I just like saying Django, because it says Django, I just like Django. Sam and I go back into the theater, the Goodman Theater. We worked together, even before that at the Negro Ensemble Company, we did a pretty good play called "A Soldier's Play," which became a great movie, "A Soldier's Story." It wasn't as good as it could have been if Sam had been involved, but that's another story. (laughs) That's for another day. What else do I have here? Lots of prizes, obviously. Big box office hit, you know all about that. Here's what you don't know. These, and there are a few, are the organizations that Samuel L. Jackson and his wife, Latonya Jackson, give to: the Alzheimer's Association, American Institute for Stuttering, American Red Cross, Artists for a New South Africa, Bedford-Stuyvesant

Restoration Corporation, Black Economic Alliance, The Brain Trust, Cedars-Sinai, Broadway Cares/Equity Fights AIDS, Carousel of Hope, Children's Defense Fund, Desmond and, and someone Tutu Legacy Foundation, Earth Island Foundation, the HollyRod Foundation for Autism and Parkinson's Disease, In a Perfect World Foundation, The Joseph Lowery Institute for Social Change, Magic Johnson Foundation, Spelman College, Morehouse College, NAACP Legal Defense Fund, National Action Network, Kidney Foundation, Solutions Coalition, the Smithsonian National Museum of African American History, Spelman College United Nero College Fund, and the Urban League. That's what he did, I don't know what you did. But that's what he did. Make sure I haven't forgotten anything.

Since we're talking about Denzel Washington, it's interesting to note that he was the third black man to win the Academy Award for Best Actor. His talent was recognized for his performance in "Training Day", a crime thriller directed by Antoine Fuqua. This happened in 2002, meaning it took Hollywood 39 years to again give the leading acting award to a black actor. Before this feat, he had already gained recognition in 1990, when he won the Academy Award for Best Supporting Actor For "Glory". Denzel Washington's trajectory in cinema is impressive, with a variety of roles in films such as "Man on Fire", "The Equalizer 1 and 2", "Fences", among others. His success reflects not only his talent of acting, but also highlights the need to recognize diversity and representation in the film industry.

Oprah Winfrey

Oprah Winfrey is an American media personality, television host, producer, actress and philanthropist, born on January 29, 1954, in Kosciusko, Mississippi. Its history is marked by challenges, successes and significant impact in the world of media. Oprah was born into a poor family. She experienced a difficult childhood, marked by poverty and traumatic episodes. At the age of nine, she was sexually abused by family members. Despite these trials, she found refuge in books and developed a love for reading and speaking. As a teenager, Oprah moved to her father's home in Nashville, Tennessee, where she began her media career. She worked in radio while still in high school, and later moved to television as a news anchor. In 1986, Oprah launched her own talk show, the "Oprah Winfrey Show". The program quickly gained popularity and became one of the most watched and influential talk shows in television history.

Oprah has spoken about a variety of topics, from mental health to interpersonal relationships, and has interviewed celebrities from around the world. Alongside her success on television, Oprah embarked on a career in film. She has been acclaimed for her performances in films such as "Color Purple" (1985), for which she was nominated for an Academy Award. Oprah has also used her fame to engage in humanitarian and philanthropic causes. She established the Oprah Winfrey Leadership Academy for Girls Foundation in South Africa, which provides educational opportunities for underprivileged girls. Oprah continued to expand her media empire by creating her own television network, OWN (Oprah Winfrey Network), in 2011. She continued to produce shows, documentaries and influence global media culture. Oprah Winfrey's story is an example of resilience, perseverance and success in the face of considerable personal challenges. She has inspired millions of people around the world, not only through her professional success, but also through her commitment to social and philanthropic causes.

REFLECTION

POSITIVE THINKING

Let's imagine if all these people, seeing the injustices of the world, and disgusted with life, took refuge in alcohol, drugs and anything that could numb them; including, according to "the evil of the century" by Châteaubriand. Let's say that Bob Marley stopped devoting himself to music and took to the streets, full of certainties and gathered with many Rastas, protested, just to shout about the real injustices that are plaguing the world, what is it what would this solve?

What are the possible outcomes of something like this?

Certainly, there would be others who praised, applauded, social networks were full of posts. The police would be there to provide security, but would soon be forced to act to suppress dissidents. Either way, we live in a generation of lots of movement, however, without quality and without functional purpose.

In fact, gays, women, Indians, and other groups feel wronged, and often in fact are. They are working tools for behavioral scientists, sociologists, politicians, etc. Not a work of improvements or responses to the demands made, but a work of manipulation and incitement to revolt, to a life of social quarrels and class conflicts. The agendas of these minority groups are like a knife, the Malian leaders go in search of cheese in the offices with which the so-called NGOs (Non-Governmental Organizations), meet those who can guarantee funds for the benefit of these peoples.

The organizations blackmail the images and threaten to send editorial staff who also receive a "handle" to produce articles. Newspaper advertisers, "committed" to the "cause", inject money into newsrooms and television channels, into factories; politicians are elected without any prior work, just to publicly say that they defend said minorities.

At the end of the process, the whole machine is lubricated with oil (silver), the gears work perfectly. The whole system is in place, but nothing has been done by those who dream of a fair world, social justice and acceptance. But that's not the worst, the real misfortune is that the one who asked for it and who didn't receive it didn't understand the maneuver. Indeed, the subtlety of the manipulator involves him with smiles, tight hugs, that "selfie" that goes on Instagram, and that incendiary speech, the most refined theater they can present.

The victim has been hearing for years:

"We work", "the white elite", the racists and blah, blah, blah.

It's a kind of mass psychosis.

When society is fragmented, everyone seeks their rights, but without intellectual unity, that is to say they are all in ecstasy, but without connection with society or with reality. This research will generate fluctuating, random anxiety, without a precise cause, so that many things no longer make sense, and it is not possible to understand them.

Automatically, the first scoundrel who poses as a leader, who gives a hopeful speech, attracts the attention of the population. It's a kind of hypnosis.

Hypnotized, they will be guided and do what the "savior" says. Sometimes people have no personal connection to the leader, they worship the speech. Reality does not concern them. Anyone who questions the manipulation is automatically labeled a fascist, a racist and so many other things.

This is "mass psychosis training."

This is exactly what happened in Germany in the 1920s, 1930s and 1940s. You know that saying about "saying what the people want to hear?"

That's it.

THE SECRET

THE SECRET

The balcony of these winners was the very high level of perceptual intelligence, but also the great personal ability. They knew what it was about, they observed diligently and thoughtfully; but they did not get involved or seek help from this system as victims. They studied, they grouped together, they grew as a group; then, after having had a solid and almost indisputable basis, they appeared. However, they did not follow anyone, they were thinking spirits. They were the medicine and hope of that time.

What I mean by that is you have to have a solid educational foundation. We don't go around making "movements" without having attended compulsory school, without having read even a good book, thinking that we are going to change a system established more than two millennia ago . This will be a mass maneuver and may end up as a criminal. But let me tell you something, firstly, they had a different talent. A gift, a particularity which made them stand out and which seduced the public. Some of them started playing nylon-string guitars in the town square, playing Gun's Roses, the Rolling Stones, Michael Jackson, Louis Armstrong and others. Others began to feel the resonance of their talents in the church.

That it is a wonderful place to test your ability to stand out in society or school, by studying, answering questions and asking intelligent questions that leave teachers amazed at the thinking ability and extent of student thinking. Understood ? Nothing falls by parachute. For God's sake, don't get me wrong.

Believe in your dreams, but don't be someone who repeats meaningless phrases and expressions that are useless. Fight, study, struggle and work. Outsmart the system you face with strategy, be quieter, stay focused and resist teasing. Sometimes we learn to make noise, but we don't have good content. Instead of shouting and creating slogans, you need to create strategies. We must strengthen the morals of the next generation, but not by using the desire for revenge or separatism. We must highlight the qualities that we carry, the references that we have in our history.

Seek real knowledge, don't just listen to stories, look for reliable sources. For example, slavery in the United States and the segregation of people there have nothing to do with racism in the rest of the world. We are not the heirs of what happened or is happening. We don't need to imitate social movements if the people are not the same. Furthermore, we are a mixed people with a multiplicity of ethnic groups and, obviously, there are prejudices and insults, but this does not constitute a feeling of social segregation, the immensity of the examples cited above is precisely there to prove this. Do. Well, today, after years of the liberation of slaves, there is still a lot to repair, inequalities exist, but this is just a historical fact. There is no social engineering that deliberately prevents black people from having access to the right to education, health and employment. It is obvious that there are sometimes prejudices and racism. There are all kinds of people, including criminals. But I don't agree with the idea of "structural racism", what exists is the stubble of a society that has been damaged in the past, but which comes gradually, as Bob said Marley,

"We will advance triumphantly in this generation" (Redemption Songs).

We reach this generation triumphantly.

So it's a waste of time, and it embarrasses the people of today, our compatriots, who have nothing to do with the things of the past.

It's as if we tendencies hand to the Germans to ask or demand social reparation for Hitler having caused the misery he caused to the Jews. Surely, a global "Jewish Lives Matter" movement should be created, you know?

We are in no way going to deny what happened, nor are we going to accept, under any circumstances, any expression of racism against black people, black people or whatever you like to be called. It is about remaining vigilant and vehemently denouncing specific racist manifestations around the world.

There is no tolerance for such social atrocity in the 21st century. However, let's not make it a flag of social solidarity. It is our culture, our talent and our competence that must be recognized, not because of our amount of melanin. Not because of our hair type.

To meditate:

– The best football player of all time was a black man.
– The best boxer of all time was a black man.
– The greatest basketball player of all time was a black man, the best and fastest runner in the world was a black man.
– The best Jazz, Soul and Gospel singers were and are black.
– Wonderful filmmakers like **Morgan Freeman, Will Smith, Cuba Gooding Jr, Eddie Murphy**.
– Other personalities like **Nelson Mandela**, one of the most emblematic figures of the fight against apartheid in South Africa. After 27 years in prison, he became the country's first black president in 1994.
– **Thurgood Marshall,**
– the first African-American justice of the United States Supreme Court. A renowned lawyer, he played a key role in the historic victory of Brown v. Board of Education, which ended racial segregation in American schools.

– Without forgetting black women like **Whoopi Goldberg, Maya Angelou** (an American writer, poet and civil rights activist).
His autobiography,"I Know Why the Caged Bird Sings", has been acclaimed and has been an influential voice in promoting social justice and equality.
– **Condoleezza Rice**, American politician and diplomat who was the first black woman to serve as United States Secretary of State. She played a key role in the formulation of American foreign policy...

Given that star rating, where would the argument for structural racism be?

And this, we are talking about a society which, until our days, there are strong presences of prejudices; American company. If we talk about Brazil, things get even more complicated. There are countless examples of people past and present, who stand out in society, all black and mixed race.

I am aware that many black activists use the agenda intelligently, that is, they want to prevent it from falling into oblivion, and that the leftovers increase and become normalized in today's society 'today; It's a valid strategy.

However, anyone participating in the "movement" must be informed of the true goal. Otherwise, they imply limiting beliefs in the impending youth who fall into a religion and even a revolutionary movement. This may seem exaggerated, but we are a very warm, very passionate people. Which is very easily divided into dichotomies, us versus them.

My invitation is a desire to make friends who escape these segregationist lines, even if I understand that the supporters do not do it on purpose.

One example that I cannot fail to address before ending this conversation concerns "racial quotas." Look: our people are divided into social classes, not by color.

There are rich blacks, poor Indians, middle-class mixed race people and white beggars. The issue is therefore social. If the intention is to fight inequality, quotas must be social and not racial.

Think with me:

 Let's imagine that a law is created, in which it is established that each university reserves **20 %** of each course to those who benefit from social quotas. Under this plan, anyone with an income below two minimum wages could register and compete for a place at university.

Soon, Indians, blacks, whites, browns, yellows, greens and blues could register. So, since the lower class is very diverse, this would prevent a prejudiced fool from using, in the future, the argument: "**you only got this far because you had a scholarship, it wasn't merit, it was charity** ". Since the law would be so plural, it would cover everyone.

On the other hand, if the law only benefits black people, this identification would be much more obvious and would perpetuate in society the feeling of inferiority among black people themselves and of superiority and disdain among the marginal executives who believe himself to be superior. This would already start with HR reviewing the candidate's curriculum. The photo of the black candidate, combined with the quota college from which he graduated, would already be either grounds for rejecting the application or grounds for proposals to lower salaries.

Let's imagine that this candidate is in a company where everyone is trained by merit in private colleges, only this black person is there because he benefits from "remedial action from the State", "affirmative action", obviously , the feeling of inferiority arises. This is what, as a black person, I diametrically disagree with. For me, everyone, from the poor class, deserves the right to receive an education, gays, whites, Indians, men, women, everyone should have access to social quotas.

I want to leave a personal example, I think my reader deserves it:

In 1994, I qualified as a carpenter, in a course taken atLar Fabiano de Cristo,"Capemi" has Alto de Coutos, Salvador-Bahia. The teacher was a white guy, Antonio Carlos, boring and quite demanding. It was embodied in me, because I loved making parts, but I didn't like being millimetric in measurements, which left the parts out of square. The teacher got angry, and I thought it was funny.

About that, Rosealves, a guy living in Paripe, he was a phenomenal young man. He took great care in measuring and finishing the pieces, as well as in the varnishing. I got my certificate, because of my mother who made these threats and because of the teacher. Even so, Rosealves was the best student in the course. He was black.

In this same course I learned to carve wood and make names and images to put on bars, bedroom doors, in short, wood crafts. That interested me more than making furniture.

While making a chisel at home with an umbrella iron, my brothers were impressed and called my mother to watch. She, a little surprised, asked me how I had done it and what I needed to buy a briefcase. I detailed everything and, even with limited financial conditions, my father purchased a complete set. It was great, everyone wanted me to name their son to be paid at the end of the month etc.

However, the money did not come in, the work required sandpaper, gouache, varnish and staples. And my father gave me the idea to go to «Market », the historic center of Salvador.

When I arrived there, with my pieces, I saw the grandeur of the works of art exhibited there. I saw the professionalism of the artists and their stands, all organized and with artistic ownership. I was sixteen.

Furthermore, I remember looking and turning between the **Lacerda elevator (tourist point)**, the Market Model and the Brazilian Navy.

Literally lost, not knowing what to do. I took courage and asked a "rasta" in a tent how I should go about working on it at their place. He laughingly explained to me that I was a minor and that I couldn't work there. According to him, I should grow up and after refining my work, I could rent a stand at the town hall. There were only black people there. I just wasn't prepared.

I went to sell ice lollies in the street, on buses, on the beach. Likewise, I took an automobile mechanics course for light and heavy vehicles at one of the best institutes in Brazil, if not the best, SENAI.

How did I get in?

I entered a selection competition, thanks to the fact that I was a street vendor at the time.

On the day of the test, there were white, of the blondes, of the **Galician**, of the **Indians** and one **brun** who lived on a street below mine, and I was surprised to find him, because he was training sponsored by UNICEF and I thought his family had money, it was Ivanildo. A few days later the result came out, I was approved.

For me, incredible! Me, David Amorim and Ivanildo, the toothy guy from the other street, competed for the title of best in class. So, in all humility, I'm so boring, of course it was me. The professor, a very competent black man, with a big eye the size of a billiard ball, a well-spoken voice and a helpful sense of humor. When I graduated I was already 18 years and a few months old, I had done it in February and the course finished in August of that year. Even so, one of the electronic injection professors opened an internship opportunity for me at Indiana Vehicles, but I had to go through a test.

 I remember I got there early, waited about 50 minutes and one guy told me to come in, then another young man came in, brown hair, yellow skin, had experience with his dad at the workshop, but had never taken a course. We chatted for a while and were called to speak to a man. I didn't know how to read (English) the information that was on a yellow plate, written in black letters, it was information on the car's engine. Many of the details of those who had daily practical experience I did not have. Elton got the job and as a consolation the man told me he was going to keep my CV.

Since then, I have already been a salesman in shoe stores, a radio and promotions presenter in supermarkets. I was a machine operator, I'm a mason. I worked as an assembler and boilermaker-plumber at Petrobras, I was a traveling salesman, in my town and throughout Brazil. Furthermore, I was an English teacher in primary school, took many technical courses, trained in telemarketing and participated in a difficult selection to work at Banco do Brasil. I have a bachelor's degree in theology from Brazil and another from abroad. In 2012, I founded a community association in Switzerland, or chair until today. I have written a lot of books, including in other languages.

I currently work on migration security in Switzerland, I speak several languages and scratch in others. Not only that, but I work with people from Senegal, Uganda, Togo, Nigeria, Congo, Ivory Coast and Cameroon. All black winners, who migrated and believed in the realization of dreams. Today, living in Europe for more than twelve years, I am certain that effort, discipline and preparation bear fruit at the right time. At some point, something has to happen. Even if it does not materialize 100%, if we start from zero, from the state of discredit and, if we take a step, it is already a great success. Our children, certainly influenced by our trajectory, will take other steps, our grandchildren will certainly get there. If we're the ones who made it, so much the better. I believe in god. I believe you!

Go, fight, conquer, then come back and tell your story.

COMMENTS

COMMENTS

The strength of the spirit!

Black people don't commit suicide.

Black people are born brave.

The black man is the first human being on earth.

They have been through everything in their lives.

They have a heart and get whatever they want, whenever they want.

Black is synonymous with power.

Moussa Diallo-Baol, *Senegal (Bienne, Bern-Switzerland)*

Dear Sérgio, I thank you for reminding us of black people who fight every day at all levels to be the best in each discipline, in order to silence criticism linked to racial discrimination.

Touré Christopher-France

I would like to thank Sérgio for this work, which I really appreciated. You know, most physically and mentally strong black people are people who don't wait for the solution to come from outside.

These are people who set themselves the goal of succeeding, regardless of their religious affiliation, ethnicity or origin.

Hiding behind your skin color to harm others is wickedness and human weakness.

For me, everything is a question of will, courage and decision to become "victorious" as the title of the work says. Whether we are black or white. You cannot be born strong, you become strong with time and experience.

Falikou Thea - Republic of Guinea

MIXED PEOPLE

"Hey you, naked man, house without doors, crown of feathers.

Do you know that they do not want your best, that what is stopping you comes from a stratagem?

Well, they've been pushing you into the nest for a while, they're making you a shield.

They take advantage of your little education, they say what they will be, teaching it to be silent.

So like the white people came, showed you mirrors and stole everything.

Now you're on TV, the appeal is to keep your butt bare.

You could be rich, raise your kid and why not your Nico.

But something far from the forest is destroying your party since the day of the party.

Maybe your peaceful life out there in the woods keeps you from getting there.

In another system, internet and antenna, education and progress.

Listen, honorable cacique, inert, don't stay on this stick and this cob.

I respect your position, your conviction, your experience, your objective, explain to me.

Why so much forest and mud, without sustenance for the tribe and for those you love.

These lands, oh my nobility, of such beauty, could be the Bahamas.

Try to mingle with us, be independent, come and prosper.

No longer be the target of NGOs like ping-pong who want to exploit you.

Don't let yourself be lured by another nation either, the forest is the aquarium.

Who guards animals with arrows, in the time of guns, the Hilarious.

This mania for shortening the expression, dwarf culture, priest's tale.

It's the guarantee of money, people who breastfeed, benefit from documentaries.

Come and teach us your cure, and we will teach you how to grow coffee.

Although we do not speak your language, we wanted your secrets and to teach you our faith.

You too, iron muscular, resistant to the sun, eyes of candor.

Have you noticed that you harbor insecurity within yourself because your skin is dark?

Well, this vile subject cannot be weighted down, nor can I choose a chair for you.

Don't let them see you, just talk about sadness and capoeira.

Not that the subject is shameful, or that the subject is always pejorative.

It's just that tanned skin belongs to workers and also to managers.

The sailor who gave you so much work played a game of marked cards.

However, the moment is different, the pain has gone down the drain, it is recovery.

Force coming from a land, from the valley, from the mountains, from the occult force.

From the lactating breast, without knowing if the child would become an adult.

From lack of breast milk, infernal heat, killing malaria.

Overcame so many difficulties, arrived in the city, crossed the sea.

Why let pennies enslave you and bring you agony?

Power, beauty and irony, the gift of Africa has arrived in Bahia.

And you, cold white, which in the sun turns red like a shrimp.

You, European eye, join him and me and let us be brothers.

It's time to unite without fights, boys and girls and the undecided too.

Whether it's a Catholic Church, a spiritualist church or just rhetoric, amen.

Who builds something alone, without talking to the neighbor, without advice?

Let's go out together now, at the new dawn, all for the Nation.

As the division of captaincies ended a few days ago, the turtle succumbed.

Currently, we are a country admired, known and envied, we are the WORLD.

END

Book written in January 2024, Noiraigue, Switzerland.

About the Author

Born in Salvador, Bahia, Sergio Junior is a man with a hybrid soul and a proactive spirit. He communicates in a way that resolves conflict and leads to reflection. An excellent analytical mind, he interacts with the interlocutor in a serene and voluntary manner. In October 2011, Sérgio had a near-death experience, which gave him a new meaning to life on this level.

A true advisor, he writes on human behavior, emotional intelligence and analytical psychology; has published books in France, Portugal and Brazil. He founded the association IEME in Switzerland and works in immigration security in the same country where he has lived since 2011. Pragmatic and poetic, he draws attention to his bionic writing method; natural and spiritual. In 2019, he won the "Psalms Moderns III" poetry competition in Boston in the United States. In 2020 and 2021 he finished second in the "Best of Brazil in Europe" award as the best Brazilian writer. The awards ceremony took place in London at Kensington Palace. His way of thinking about the world is already known to readers on social networks and in published books. Among the books he wrote is the magnificent work launched by Librinova:**"I was at your funeral"**, published in Portuguese in Paraná-Brazil by the publishing house CRV, which gave the author national notoriety. The work in French was published by Librinova. He also chairs a social missionary project in several districts of Nacala-Porto Mozambique.

Other books by the author:

Sergio Junior(uiclap.bio)

Contacts :

00 21 + 41 78 731 38 21

Instagram.com/escritorsergiojunior

poderdesintese@protonmail.com

https://www.facebook.com/livrariasergiojunior/shop/

Thanks

Gratitude is my motto in my life, which is why I extend it to my readers, friends and family, for their tireless and motivating support. To all those who, during all these years, have been directly and indirectly a source of inspiration in this other part of my life, artistic, social and cultural.

Feel embraced in this work.

Sergio Junior

www.ingramcontent.com/pod-product-compliance
Lightning Source LLC
Chambersburg PA
CBHW070950260726
48661CB00003B/1215